BRONTË
WUTHERING HEIGHTS

Continuum *Reader's Guides*

Continuum Reader's Guides are clear, concise and accessible introductions to classic literary texts. Each book explores the themes, context, criticism and influence of key works, providing a practical introduction to close reading and guiding the reader towards a thorough understanding of the text. Ideal for undergraduate students, the guides provide an essential resource for anyone who needs to get to grips with a literary text.

Achebe's *Things Fall Apart* – Ode Ogede
Atwood's *The Handmaid's Tale* – Gina Wisker
Austen's *Emma* – Gregg A. Hecimovich
Borges' *Short Stories* – Rex Butler
Bram Stoker's *Dracula* William Hughes
Bronte's *Jane Eyre* Zoe Brennan
Chaucer's *The Canterbury Tales* – Gail Ashton
Conrad's *Heart of Darkness* – Allan Simmons
Dickens's *Great Expectations* – Ian Brinton
Eliot's *Middlemarch* – Josie Billington
Fitzgerald's *The Great Gatsby* – Nicolas Tredell
Fowles's *The French Lieutenant's Woman* – William Stephenson
Hardy's *Tess of the D'Urbervilles* – Greg Hardy
James's *The Turn of the Screw* – Leonard Orr
Joyce's *Ulysses* – Sean Sheehan
Salinger's *The Catcher in the Rye* – Sarah Graham
Shelley's *Frankenstein* – Graham Allen
William Blake's *Poetry* – Jonathan Roberts
Woolf's *To the Lighthouse* – Janet Winston

BRONTË'S
WUTHERING HEIGHTS

A READER'S GUIDE

IAN BRINTON

continuum

Continuum International Publishing Group
The Tower Building   80 Maiden Lane,
11 York Road   Suite 704
London SE1 7NX   New York, NY 10038

www.continuumbooks.com

© Ian Brinton 2010

Ian Brinton has asserted his right under the Copyright, Designs and Patents Act, 1988, to be identified as Author of this work.

British Library Cataloguing-in-Publication Data
A catalogue record for this book is available from the British Library.

ISBN: 978–1–8470–6456–1 (hardcover)
ISBN: 978–1–8470–6457–8 (paperback)

Library of Congress Cataloging-in-Publication Data
A catalog record of this book is available from the Library of Congress.

Typeset by Newgen Imaging Systems Pvt. Ltd, Chennai, India.
Printed and bound in India by Replika Press Pvt Ltd

CONTENTS

CHAPTER 1

CONTEXTS

Emily Brontë was born in July 1818 at Thornton in the parish of the West Yorkshire industrial town of Bradford. Her father, Patrick, became curate of the church at Haworth, some 8 miles away, in 1820 and moved into the Parsonage with his wife and five young children. However, within 18 months of making the move a sixth child, Anne, had been born, and the children's mother died in agonizing pain from uterine cancer, leaving the young family to be brought up under the eagle eye of their aunt, Miss Elizabeth Branwell, who transferred her home from Penzance to the bleak Yorkshire moors surrounding the black stone town of Haworth. Katherine Frank's account of this moment in the lives of the Brontë children emphasizes the difficulties felt by the young children at this stage of life:

> Isolated as they were, and intimidated too by the coldness of their aunt and their father, the six children had only each other to cling to. They knew death too young, they learned helplessness and emotional starvation too early. Despite the two grown-ups who saw to their physical and educational needs, they had become with Maria Brontë's death permanent orphans. And here we glimpse already the origin of the themes of abandonment, victimization and exile which permeate all of Emily Brontë's writing. (Frank p. 41)

In 1825, the two elder girls, Maria and Elizabeth, both died of tuberculosis contracted while at the grimly run school at Cowan Bridge. The harsh regime of training at this Clergy Daughters' School became a central feature of the early parts of Charlotte Brontë's novel, *Jane Eyre*, and the death of the gifted Maria, who had become almost like a surrogate mother to the younger children, left an indelible mark on the minds of the others. Maria was 11 years old when she died, and she was buried on Ascension Day next to her mother in the vault beneath Haworth Church. According to Winifred Gérin:

> Branwell, a strong new influence on the sisters just returned from school, with his ghoulish imaginings, declared characteristically that he heard Maria's voice crying outside the windows at night. (Gérin p. 10)

A haunting echo of this appears in Chapter 3 of *Wuthering Heights* when Lockwood dreams of breaking the windowpane so that he can stop the fir-bough knocking against it, only to discover that his fingers 'closed on the fingers of a little, ice-cold hand!' Trapped in the nightmare he has a sight of 'a child's face looking through the window'. It becomes clear that this image of existence outside the window was something shared by all three sisters 20 years after the deaths of the two elder children. Whereas Emily Brontë's reference has an almost visceral nightmare Gothicism to it, Charlotte's William Crimsworth in *The Professor* 'often heard at night the tapping of branches against the panes' in his Brussels boarding school. Unable to see into the garden where the 'demoiselles' play, he longed to tear down the dividing shutters in order to 'get a glimpse of the green region which I imagined to lie beyond'. One of Jane Eyre's water-colour paintings, which she shows to Mr. Rochester at Thornfield Hall, reveals 'a drowned corpse glanced through the green water'. A little like Catherine Earnshaw reaching out to the social world of the inside as she gives her 'doleful cry moaning on' this corpse has 'a fair arm', which 'was the only limb clearly visible, whence the bracelet had been washed or torn'. The haunting prevalence of this image of the dead trying to break through the barrier which lies between past and present became evident to Mrs. Gaskell whose *Life of Charlotte Bronte* had been commissioned by

Patrick, the patriarchal survivor, soon after the death of his sole remaining child in March 1855. Mrs. Gaskell described Charlotte Brontë's feelings after the deaths of the remaining siblings, Branwell, Emily and Anne, as she herself concentrated upon writing the early chapters of *Shirley*:

> She went on with her work steadily. But it was dreary to write without anyone to listen to the progress of her tale – to find fault or to sympathise – while pacing the length of the parlour in the evenings, as in the days that were no more. Three sisters had done this – then two, the other sister dropping off from the walk – and now one was left desolate, to listen for echoing steps that never came, and to hear the wind sobbing at the windows, with an almost articulate sound. (Gaskell p. 303)

Early on in her biography, Mrs. Gaskell gave an account of the life and society in Haworth, which provided the background for the growing Brontë children. She referred to the local inhabitants as possessing a 'remarkable degree of self-sufficiency', which gave them 'an air of independence rather apt to repel a stranger':

> Indeed, there is little display of any of the amenities of life among this wild, rough population. Their accost is curt; their accent and tone of speech blunt and harsh. Something of this may, probably, be attributed to the freedom of mountain air and of isolated hill-side life…(Gaskell p. 8)

She also referred to the bearing of grudges, 'in some cases amounting to hatred', which could continue from one generation to the next:

> I remember Miss Bronte once telling me that it was a saying round about Haworth, 'Keep a stone in thy pocket seven year; turn it, and keep it seven year longer, that it

may be ever ready to thine hand when thine enemy draws near.' (Gaskell p. 9)

The deaths of the two elder girls, Maria and Elizabeth, in 1825 had a profound effect upon the remaining four children, and motherless children and orphans became a feature which haunted the novels of both Charlotte and Emily Brontë. Juliet Barker points out that not only does virtually every child in *Wuthering Heights* lose at least one parent, usually the mother, but also that 'the relationship between the two cousins, Linton and Catherine, particularly, is essentially that of a mother surrogate and her child.'

The imaginative world of the Brontë children was intense and prompted both by their reading and their use of toy wooden soldiers they made up and acted out plays which became increasingly involved with a complex saga, the imaginary Glass Town Federation situated in the Ashantee country of West Africa. Charlotte and Branwell developed the plots into a story of the kingdom of Angria.

In January 1831, Charlotte left home to go to school at Roe Head, some 20 miles away near Huddersfield, leaving Emily to sleep on her own for the first time, and the younger girl's growing sense of independence was further extended by her breaking away from the dominance of Charlotte and Branwell's Angrian world to create her own imaginary world of Gondal along with her younger sister Anne. Whereas the earlier imaginary island had been dominated by the so-called Glass Town Chronicles, Emily's new part of the fictional world was dominated by the moors surrounding Haworth. As Winifred Gérin points out, the two younger girls spent a considerable amount of time outside:

The poetry of Gondal, like Scott's and the Border Ballads before it, was an essentially outdoor creation, depending on landscape for its major effects. The more closely Emily and Anne grew to know the changing aspects of the moors in all seasons, the vegetation with its brilliant annual return of blushing bilberry leaves, hare-bells, heath, and bracken; to watch for and closely observe the swift changes of clouds and wind-directions which their position high up on a spur of the Pennines, between two nearby coasts, provoked; the more they identified themselves with the reckless actions of their outlaws and rebels fleeing from justice, or from pursuing armies, and sheltering in the hollows of rocks or down in the glens which were their secret haunts – the more Gondal grew. (Gérin p. 26)

Emily was allowed exceptional liberty for the time, and the only stipulation about rambling on the moors was that she and Anne should be accompanied either by their elder brother, Branwell, or by Tabitha Aykroyd who had been employed since 1824 as servant in the Bronte household. 'Tabby' was 56 years old when she first joined the family and was well known for being a 'joined Methodist' whose own memories of the local area stretched back to the 1780s.

At the end of July 1835, Emily left home for the first time since her brief time at Cowan Bridge. Charlotte had accepted a teaching post at Roe Head, and Emily accompanied her to become a full-time student at the school. The arrangement only lasted a few months on account of Emily's feelings of extreme homesickness. Charlotte expressed the sense of disjunction in her sister's life in a 'Prefatory Note to Selections from Poems by Ellis Bell':

Liberty was the breath of Emily's nostrils; without it, she perished. The change from her own home to a school, and from her own very noiseless, very secluded, but unrestricted and inartificial mode of life, to one of disciplined routine (though under the kindliest auspices) was what she failed of enduring. Her nature here proved too strong for fortitude. Every morning when she woke, the vision of home and the moors rushed on her. Nobody knew what ailed her but me. I knew only too well. In this struggle her health was quickly broken: her white face, attenuated form, and failing strength threatened rapid decline. I felt in my heart she would die if she did not go home, and with this conviction, obtained her recall.

For the next 2 years, Emily remained at home in Haworth with her aunt and father and Branwell whose own attempt at success in London had been doomed to ignominious failure. Having made the 2-day journey to the capital in order to start a career as an artist he appears to have spent about a week at the Chapter Coffee House in Paternoster Row before returning home penniless and without either the letters of recommendation or the sketchbook of drawings he had taken with him.

During the time at home now, Emily began writing the poems which are associated with the world of Gondal, and her urgent need for freedom can be felt from the earliest drafts. A poem from December 1836 opens

> High waving heather, 'neath stormy blasts bending,
> Midnight and moonlight and bright shining stars;
> Darkness and glory rejoicingly blending,
> Earth rising to heaven and heaven descending,
> Man's spirit away from its drear dongeon sending,
> Bursting the fetters and breaking the bars.

References to winds, breezes and blasts occur in more than half of Emily's poems, and on 17 occasions they appear in the first line.

In the autumn of 1838, Emily took up the post of resident teacher at Law Hill, 8 miles away from Haworth. The school, owned and run by Miss Patchett, stood some 1,000 feet up under the summit of Beacon Hill, and it looked out over open moorland. The curious history of the house itself became part of the thematic background to *Wuthering*

Heights. The long hours and the uncongenial work prompted
Charlotte to write:

> Emily is gone into a situation as a teacher in a large school
> of near forty pupils, near Halifax. I have had one letter
> from her since her departure; it gives an appalling account
> of her duties – hard labour from six in the morning until
> near eleven at night, with only one half-hour of exercise
> between. This is slavery. I fear she will never stand it.

Her homesickness and the unyielding responsibilities of
full-time teaching led to a breakdown of health, and Emily
returned to Haworth in March – April 1839. During her time
at Law Hill, she had continued to find some relief by keeping
the world of Gondal alive and, in the winter of 1838, had written one of her most moving records of loss and yearning:

> A little while, a little while,
> The noisy crowd are barred away;
> And I can sing and I can smile –
> A little while I've holyday!
>
> Where wilt thou go my harassed heart?
> Full many a land invites thee now;
> And places near, and far apart
> Have rest for thee, my weary brow –
>
> There is a spot mid barren hills
> Where winter howls and driving rain
> But if the dreary tempest chills
> There is a light that warms again
>
> The house is old, the trees are bare
> And moonless bends the misty dome
> But what on earth is half so dear –
> So longed for as the hearth of home?

Between her return to Haworth in the spring of 1839 and
her enthusiastic embracing of her sisters' scheme in July
1841 to set up their own school, Emily wrote upwards of

50 poems and verse fragments, which have survived, as well as Gondal prose works, which are lost. Katherine Frank describes the method of working at her writing as 'piecemeal but careful':

> She would scribble first drafts on any scraps of paper which came to hand, while in the midst of tidying the parlour or peeling potatoes or kneading bread in the kitchen, for her head was often full of phrases of verse, metaphors, images, scenes or Gondal events. In the evenings, after her father and aunt retired, Emily would take out her lap desk and systematically rework and revise the fragments of verse she had jotted down in the course of the day. (Frank p. 145–6)

One aspect of this manner of working finds a counterpart in the young Catherine Earnshaw's jotting down of notes in the margins of her small library of books discovered by Lockwood in his room within a room when he spends the night at Wuthering Heights:

> Catherine's library was select, and its state of dilapidation proved it to have been well used, though not altogether for a legitimate purpose; scarcely one chapter had escaped a pen-and-ink commentary – at least, the appearance of one – covering every morsel of blank that the printer had left. (p. 20)

Of this writing, 'some were detached sentences; other parts took the form of a regular diary.'

To further the scheme of opening their own school, Charlotte's friend, Mary Taylor, suggested that the sisters should spend some time improving their languages by studying in Brussels. There would be the added advantage of widening their cultural education as a preparation for opening their own Boarding establishment. Aunt Branwell put up the money, and Emily was persuaded to join Charlotte in their departure for Brussels in February 1842 accompanied by Patrick Brontë.

While in Brussels, Emily wrote only two poems, which perhaps is a reflection upon the amount of time she had to use in order to cope with the learning of lessons in French. Her forthright, even stubborn, character became evident in her reaction to her teacher's suggestion that she should write some imitative composition exercises, which she saw as resulting in the loss of originality in thought and expression. In this light, M. Heger's assessment of her character is revealing:

> She should have been a man – a great navigator. Her powerful reason would have deduced new spheres of discovery from the knowledge of the old; and her strong, imperious will would never have been daunted by opposition or difficulty; never have given way but with life. (Barker p. 392)

Juliet Barker comments on her intractable nature in Brussels where 'She not only seems to have set out with absolutely no intention of making friends, but was so uncompromisingly self-centred that she incurred positive dislike.' In the essays she wrote for M. Heger, there is a sharp-edged directness, which ignores any Victorian sentimentality, and in 'The Butterfly', she can conclude with an eloquent statement of Christian belief having written earlier that 'Nature is an inexplicable problem; it exists on a principle of destruction' where 'everything must be a tireless instrument of death to others or else cease to live itself.' In the essay, she pauses to look at a beautiful flower before recognizing that its centre has been eaten by a caterpillar, which she then, in disgust, treads underfoot. It is only as she sees a butterfly that she realizes that 'The created should not judge his Creator.'

The death of Aunt Branwell in autumn of 1842 compelled the sisters to return to Haworth where Emily discovered that her aunt had disposed of the two geese and the hawk, Hero, which had been family pets. While Charlotte returned to Brussels, Branwell joined Anne at Thorp Green in order to tutor the Robinson household, leaving Emily in sole charge of the house where she remained for the rest of her short life.

In February 1844, Emily began to collect together her poems in order to bring them into two notebooks, one with the title 'Gondal Poems' and the other untitled, and it was one of these that Charlotte discovered in 1845 when she 'accidentally lighted on a M.S. volume of verse in my sister Emily's handwriting. Recognizing the 'peculiar music' of these poems, 'wild, melancholy, and elevating', Charlotte took the lead in putting them together with her own and the youngest sister Anne's for publication. Emily felt that her privacy had been invaded, and it was some time before the initial rift was healed after two concessions to publication had been extracted from Charlotte: the removal of references to the world of Gondal and the use of pseudonyms for publication. Emily's contribution to *Poems by Currer, Ellis and Acton Bell* was 21 poems, 14 of which had been written within the last 2 years. Charlotte's assessment of the worth of these poems was significant:

> I know – no woman that ever lived – ever wrote such poetry before – Condensed energy, clearness, finish – strange, strong pathos are their characteristics – utterly different from the weak diffusiveness – the laboured yet most feeble wordiness which dilute the writings of even very popular poetesses. (*The Brontës* II p. 256)

The complete commercial failure of *Poems*, of which only two copies were sold, was no setback for the Brontë sisters in terms of their novel writing, and on 6 April 1846 Charlotte had communicated to Aylott and Jones that 'C.E & A. Bell are now preparing for the Press a work of fiction – consisting of three distinct and unconnected tales which may be published either together as a work of 3 vols. of the ordinary novel-size, or separately as single vols.' The three 'tales' which were written during the winter and spring of 1845–1846 were *The Professor*, *Wuthering Heights* and *Agnes Grey*, although the last two didn't find a publisher until June 1847 and *The Professor* only appeared after Charlotte's death. No manuscript survives to give an exact date of the composition of *Wuthering Heights*, although the actual writing appears to have started by October 1845. The publisher Thomas Cautley Newby agreed to publish the finished novel in July 1847, but it was only after Smith Elder's overwhelming success with *Jane Eyre* in October that he pushed the venture forward. Newby's public assertion that all the Bell novels, including *The Tenant of Wildfell Hall*, were the creations of the author of *Jane Eyre* prompted Charlotte and Anne to go to London to make themselves known. Emily declined to go, and the depth of her resentment at having her true identity revealed is registered in the letter which Charlotte sent on 31 July 1848 to W. S. Williams, the literary adviser to Smith, Elder:

Permit me to caution you not to speak of sisters when you write to me. I mean, do not use the word in the plural. Ellis Bell will not endure to be alluded to under any other appellation than the nom de plume. I committed a grand error in betraying his identity to you and Mr. Smith. It was inadvertent – the words 'we are three sisters' escaped me before I was aware. I regretted the avowal the moment I had made it; I regret it bitterly now, for I find it is against every feeling and intention of Ellis Bell. (Brontës II p. 240)

Emily Brontë's fierce independence of character remained with her until her death from pulmonary tuberculosis at the age of 30 in December 1848.

STUDY QUESTIONS

1. Emily Bronte's home in Haworth Parsonage seems to be of central importance to her. How can you relate this sense of 'home' to your reading of *Wuthering Heights*?

2. The biographical details of Emily Bronte's life suggest that she was a deeply private individual. In what ways can you relate this world of privacy and secrecy to your reading of the novel?

3. Emily Bronte's early personal experience of death made a great impression on her. How is this reflected in *Wuthering Heights*?

CHAPTER 2

LANGUAGE, STYLE AND FORM

There is very little original material of Emily Brontë's in existence and therefore any real sense of the literary background to *Wuthering Heights* is dependent upon the letters and comments of Charlotte. For instance, only three letters of Emily's have survived as opposed to some six or seven hundred of Charlotte's. In addition to this literary vacuum, there is no manuscript for *Wuthering Heights* and no record of the author's early writings: they have disappeared along with the prose chronicles of Gondal.

Remarking on this in *The Birth of Wuthering Heights*, Edward Chitham comments 'It is perhaps surprising to discover no notes on the novel, no first drafts, no outlines of plot.' However, he does proceed to give an account of what does remain:

> Surveying Emily's remaining manuscript output we find a host of poem manuscripts, some small pieces of paper on which single day journals or diaries have been written, drawings and sketches, the remains of an account book, some *Devoirs* done in Belgium, a tiny clutch of short letters, a very few short notes or lists attached to poems or found with poems, names and annotations in music books and possibly some marks on blotting paper. There is very little else, and these pieces are sometimes very damaged, very small and almost illegible. (Chitham p. 8)

The manuscript of Charlotte Bronte's *The Professor*, which was presented for possible publication, at the same time does, however, exist, and it is possible to conjecture that the script for Emily Brontë's novel would have been presented to the publishers in a similar format. Perhaps we can guess at one aspect of what early drafts of *Wuthering Heights* may have appeared like from Chitham's analysis of the 1837 diary paper revealing close connections with the diary style of filling paper found in the books looked at by Lockwood in the Heights bedroom. This style includes caricature drawings and is worked on small scraps of paper:

> Doubtless part of the reason for such parsimony was the cost of paper, but there is a secretive air about Emily Brontë's writing which is underlined by this host of tiny leaves. (Chitham p. 15)

However, to add to our understanding of the way in which Emily worked, Charlotte's correspondence and her detailed conversations with Mrs. Elizabeth Gaskell have left a clear picture of the life in the Haworth Parsonage and, most importantly, the literary interests of the three novelist sisters.

THE INFLUENCE OF SIR WALTER SCOTT
On 4 July 1834, Charlotte Brontë wrote to her friend Ellen Nussey offering advice about what should be read for one's education. Among the poets, it comes as no surprise to see the names of Shakespeare, Milton, Scott and Byron. At this point, Charlotte adds the comment:

> Now Ellen don't be startled at the names of Shakespeare and Byron. Both these were great men and their works are like themselves. (*The Brontës* I p. 122)

When it came to novel reading, the advice was uncompromising:

> For fiction – read Scott alone; all novels after his are worthless. (ibid.)

Sir Walter Scott's rise to popularity came initially through his poetry with the publication in 1802–1803 of a collection

Minstrelsy of the Scottish Border, and the Brontë family were avid readers of this poetry. One particular favourite was 'The Lay of the Last Minstrel', much of which they learned by heart from Patrick Brontë's 1806 edition, which he had purchased while at Cambridge. Both the poetry and the novels were particular favourites of Emily, and in December 1827, she chose Scott to be her chief man and Arran to be her island in the play 'Tales of the Islanders'. When the world of Gondal was being created, the landscape which dominated the poetry reflected Emily's reading as much as it did the moorland surrounding Haworth. In her comprehensive account of the lives of the Brontës, Juliet Barker refers specifically to Scott's novel *Rob Roy*, first published in 1819, as being the book which haunts the world of *Wuthering Heights*:

> *Wuthering Heights* which, ironically, is regarded as the archetypal Yorkshire novel, was actually Gondal through and through and therefore owed as much, if not more, to Walter Scott's Border country as to Emily's beloved moorlands of home. Echoes of his novel *Rob Roy*, for instance, are to be found throughout the book. In *Wuthering Heights*, one is irresistibly reminded of *Rob Roy*'s setting in the wilds of Northumberland, among the uncouth and quarrelsome squirearchical Osbaldistones, who spend their time drinking and gambling. The spirited and wilful Cathy has strong similarities with Diana Vernon, who is equally out of place among her boorish relations. Heathcliff, whose unusual name recalls that of the surly Thorncliff, mimics Rashleigh Osbaldistone in his sinister hold over the Earnshaws and Lintons and his attempt to seize their inheritances. (Barker p. 501)

Scott's influence can be felt early on in *Rob Roy* where Frank Osbaldistone arrives in the north of England in 'the geography of the unknown land', a country in which he is 'wrecked'.

As Rashleigh points out to him, there is a significant difference between a romanticized view of the world into which he has come and its harsh actuality:

> ... it is no isle of Calypso, umbrageous with shade and intricate with sylvan labyrinth, but a bare ragged Northumbrian moor, with as little to interest curiosity as to delight the eye – you may descry it in all its nakedness in half an hour's survey, as well as if I were to lay it down before you by rule and compass. (*Rob Roy* p. 95)

Lockwood's opening comments in *Wuthering Heights* reflect a similar Southerner's idealized sense of what rural isolation might contain, which is later presented as a direct contrast to the stark reality of what is to be found there:

> 1801 – I have just returned from a visit to my landlord – the solitary neighbour that I shall be troubled with. This is certainly a beautiful country! In all England, I do not believe that I could have fixed on a situation so completely removed from the stir of society. A perfect misanthropist's Heaven ... (p. 3)

However, his second visit to the Heights conveys the inhospitable reality of the place in uncompromising terms where on the 'bleak hill top the earth was hard with a black frost', and having arrived at the Heights only to find the gate barred, he 'knocked vainly for admittance' until his 'knuckles tingled, and the dogs howled' (p. 9).

This sense of the bleak isolation of the Heights acting as a direct contrast to a romantic vision of what the open landscape might have to offer is also emphasized by the disillusioned Isabella whose romantic notions of passionate love with Heathcliff are soon shattered as she arrives at her marital home in the Heights:

> How did you contrive to preserve the common sympathies of human nature when you resided here? I cannot

recognise nay sentiment which those around share with me. (p. 134)

Both Wuthering Heights and Osbaldistone Hall seem to have the power to infect the behaviour of those who reside in them, exaggerating traits which already exist within characters yet perverting them by making them more extreme. In the opening chapter of *Wuthering Heights*, Lockwood informs us of his 'deliberate heartlessness' in the way he behaves towards a young lady while 'enjoying a month of fine weather at the sea-coast'. This callous social behaviour becomes shockingly physical when, staying under the roof at the Heights, he dreams of pulling the wrist of a young girl 'on to the broken pane, and rubbed it to and fro till the blood ran down and soaked the bed-clothes'. Similarly, the courteous and artistically inclined narrator in *Rob Roy* becomes the drunken figure who 'contradicted whatever was asserted, and attacked, without any respect to my uncle's table, both his politics and his religion'. In Scott's novel, Frank goes on to strike Rashleigh and has to be contained locked up in his own room. When confronted by Di Vernon in the cold light of the following morning, he offers 'as an excuse for follies I am not usually guilty of, the custom of this house and country' (p. 105).

What the figure of Heathcliff owes to that of Rashleigh Osbaldistone is evident from the opening descriptions of both, whereas his name owes something perhaps to Rashleigh's brother, Thorncliff. When Lockwood first sees his landlord, he refers to 'his black eyes' withdrawn 'so suspiciously under their brows', while beneath Rashleigh Osbaldistone's 'shaggy eye-brows' there lurks:

an expression of art and design, and, on provocation, a ferocity tempered by caution, which nature had made obvious to the most ordinary physiognomist, perhaps with the same intention that she has given the rattle to the poisonous snake. (*Rob Roy* p. 44)

In Chapter 6 of *Rob Roy*, Diana Vernon refers to the power wielded by Rashleigh within the family by telling Frank that although he is the youngest of the brothers, 'he has somehow or other got the entire management of all the others, and every one is sensible of the subjection' (p. 48). This is a man who 'had gradually insinuated himself into the management of his [father's] property'. Later, in Chapter 13, Frank goes on to refer to the power of Rashleigh's 'avarice or ambition', and this comment comes not long after another one made about the powerful and manipulating strength of this character:

> Well, Rashleigh is a man to be feared and wondered at, and all but loved; he does whatever he pleases, and makes all others his puppets.

The comparison here between Rashleigh's steady and remorseless control of the property and Heathcliff's calculating plans to take over both the Heights and the Grange is striking.

However, the connections between *Rob Roy* and *Wuthering Heights* do not rest solely with the characters of Rashleigh and Heathcliff. There are interesting parallels that can be drawn between the spirited and proud Diana Vernon and the figures of both the elder and the younger Cathy. For instance, when Catherine Earnshaw blocks Edgar's way out of the Heights as he insists upon leaving after having been slapped round the face in a fit of pique, she tells him 'You must not go!' As Edgar announces 'I'll not come here again!', Catherine changes her tone:

> Her eyes began to glisten and her lids to twinkle.
> 'And you told a deliberate untruth!' he said.
> 'I didn't!' she cried, recovering her speech. 'I did nothing deliberately – Well, go, if you please – get away! And now I'll cry – I'll cry myself sick!'

In *Rob Roy*, the young and romantically impressionable Frank feels himself deeply in love with Diana Vernon and is hurt by having discovered that not only does the young lady have a secret liaison but also that she has lied to him. As he attempts to leave the library, she stops him with the peremptory order:

'Stop, Mr Frank,' she said; 'ye're not to leave me in that way neither.'

As he is 'on the point of leaving the apartment, and breaking with her for ever, it cost her but a change of look and tone from that of real and haughty resentment, to that of kind and playful despotism...to lead me back to my seat, her willing subject, on her own hard terms.' The character of Di Vernon is seen by the Justice in *Rob Roy* as one that has been left alone 'and deserted on the face of this wide earth, and left to ride, and run, and scamper at her own silly pleasure' (p. 74). When she first meets the London visitor, she repels Frank's attempt at polite flirtation with the words:

I must inform you at once, Mr Osbaldistone, that compliments are entirely lost upon me. Do not, therefore, throw away your pretty sayings – they serve fine gentlemen who travel in the country, instead of the toys, beads, and bracelets, which navigators carry to propitiate the savage inhabitants of newly discovered countries. Do not exhaust your stock in trade – you will find natives in Northumberland to whom your fine things will recommend you – On me they are utterly thrown away, for I happen to know their real value. (*Rob Roy* p. 46)

The stock-in-trade compliments, which Lockwood attempts to bestow upon the younger Catherine, meet with a similar block as he comments upon 'an obscure cushion full of something like cats' only to discover that it was 'a heap of dead rabbits'.

The landscape itself of *Rob Roy* seems to offer a model for Emily Bronte's novel:

Our road continued to be, if possible, more waste and wild than that we had travelled in the forenoon. The few miserable hovels that shewed some marks of human habitation, were now of still rarer occurrence, and, at length, as we began to ascend a huge and uninterrupted swell of moorland, they totally disappeared.

In his 1981 introduction to the World's Classics edition of *Wuthering Heights*, Ian Jack pointed to an impressive list of similarities between that novel and *Waverley: or, 'Tis Sixty Years Since*. Referring to young Captain Waverley's arrival at the Scottish manor house, Jack points to an interesting comparison between the architectural description of that place and Lockwood's account of his arrival at the Heights. Edward Waverley notes the 'weather-beaten mutilated masses of upright stone' representing 'two rampant Bears', which adorn the archway to the drive leading up to the house and then proceeds to comment that the house 'seemed to consist of two or three high, narrow, and steep-roofed buildings, projecting from each other at rights angles' and that it had been built with an eye to being strongly defended:

> The windows were numberless, but very small; the roof had some nondescript kind of projections, called bartizans, and displayed at each frequent angle a small turret, rather resembling a pepper-box than a Gothic watch-tower. Neither did the front indicate absolute security from danger. There were loopholes for musketry, and iron stancheons on the lower windows, probably to repel any roving band of gipsies, or resist a predatory visit from the Caterans of the neighbouring highlands. Stables and other offices occupied another side of the square. The former were low vaults, with narrow slits instead of windows...(*Waverley* p. 38)

At the opening of the next chapter in *Waverley*, we are told that the young visitor from the South 'applied himself to the massive knocker of the hall-door, the architrave of which bore the date 1594'. On his first arrival at Wuthering Heights, Lockwood notices the exposed situation of the building and comments that 'the architect had foresight to build it strong: the narrow windows are deeply set in the wall, and the corners defended with large jutting stones.' As he halts at the threshold, he admires 'a quantity of grotesque carving lavished over the front, and especially about the principal door, above which, among a wilderness of crumbling griffins, and shameless little boys, I detected the date '1500', and the name 'Hareton Earnshaw'.

Ian Jack points to Lockwood's arrival at the Heights and his resemblance to Scott's typical young heroes – observant and educated yet also ignorant – who travel into a more primitive and violent society:

> The hero finds himself out of his depth. 'A land of enchantment have I been led into', muses the hero of *The Abbot*, 'and spells have been cast around me – every one has met me in disguise – every one has spoken to me in parables – I have been like one who walks in a weary and bewildering dream.' In *The Fortunes of Nigel* the hero reproaches himself with having become 'a mere victim of these events, which I have never even attempted to influence – a thing never acting, but perpetually acted upon'. After learning a great deal about the strange ways of the Scots at one particular point in their history the hero either marries a Scots girl or leaves Scotland to return to the South. (Jack p. x)

Ian Jack concludes that Emily Brontë 'was using one aspect of Scott's technique with considered deliberation: she was using a straightforward, naïve stranger as a visitor to a region which she knew would be new and exciting to the novel-reader of the 1840s'.

THE INFLUENCE OF BYRON
Edward Chitham refers to Emily's journal papers suggesting that they were derived from those of the poet Byron and he follows Winifred Gérin in linking them to Moore's *Life of Byron* read by the young Brontës in the 1833 edition from

Keighley Mechanics' Institute Library. Moore quotes from Byron's domestic journal, and the sparse, terse style provides an interesting comparison with Emily's creation of scene, weather and atmosphere:

> January 5th 1821 – Rose late – dull & drooping – the weather dripping & dense – Snow on the ground & Sirocco in the sky – Dined versus six o'clock – Fed the two cats, the hawk, & the tame (but not tamed) crow. (Gérin p. 38)

The brevity of this style, its ability to create tone in an almost staccato fashion, is found in the opening of the second chapter of *Wuthering Heights*:

> Yesterday afternoon set in misty and cold. I had half a mind to spend it by my study fire, instead of wading through heath and mud to Wuthering Heights. (p. 9)

This style of creating scenery with a minimum of words is found in Emily's 23rd birthday diary paper of July 1841, which is prefixed by two tiny drawings of herself. In one, she is writing by the fire, and in the second she is standing by the window looking out:

> It is Friday evening – near 9 o'clock – wild rainy weather. I am seated in the dining room/ alone/ having just concluded tidying our desk-boxes – writing this document. (Barker p. 358)

When Lockwood examines the books in the closet where he spends his night in the Heights, he discovers the pen-and-ink commentary which Catherine has added to almost every 'morsel of blank that the printer had left':

> Some were detached sentences; other parts took the form of a regular diary, scrawled in an unformed, childish hand. At the top of an extra page, quite a treasure probably when first lighted on, I was greatly amused to behold

an excellent caricature of my friend Joseph, rudely yet powerfully sketched. (p. 20)

Another effect of reading Byron's poetry may be felt in the creation of the character of Heathcliff who portrays many of the traits of the Byronic hero from both 'Manfred' (1817) and 'Cain' (1821). His arrogance and pride for instance echo Lucifer's boast to Cain:

> With us acts are exempt from time, and we
> Can crowd eternity into an hour,
> Or stretch an hour into eternity.
> (Act I, scene I, 532–4)

His confidence in his own power and importance makes him implacable when Catherine refuses to recognize these traits, and frustrated in his love, he becomes a devil. Turning on Catherine, he tells her of precisely how he feels rejected:

> And, as to you, Catherine, I have a mind to speak a few words, now, while we are at it – I want you to be aware that I *know* you have treated me infernally – infernally! Do you hear? And, if you flatter yourself that I don't perceive it you are a fool – and if you think I can be consoled by sweet words you are an idiot – and if you fancy I'll suffer unrevenged, I'll convince you of the contrary, in a very little while. (p. 111)

Never forgetting what he sees as his more than human persona, Heathcliff is outraged by what he calls Catherine's cowardly rejection of him. The outrage is like that which prompts the defeated Lucifer to tell Cain that

> Nothing can
> Quench the mind, if the mind will be itself
> And centre of surrounding things – 'tis made
> To sway. (Act I, scene I, 210–13)

The doomed and lonely Byronic hero who dominates those two dramatic poems appears perhaps as the protagonist in Emily's poem 'I am the only being whose doom' written in May 1839, where the dominant theme is the isolation and secrecy of the speaker:

> I am the only being whose doom
> No tongue would ask no eye would mourn
> I've never caused a thought of gloom
> A smile of joy since I was born
> In secret pleasure – secret tears
> This changeful life has slipped away
> As friendless after 18 years
> As lone as on my natal day

In his essay on Emily Brontë's poetry, written for the Brontë Society Transactions 1965, C. Day Lewis suggested that 'the struggle of the soul against predestined doom is one form which the freedom motif takes in Emily Brontë's work. Another is the theme of exile.' Both this struggle and the sense of exile haunt Byron's 'Manfred' whose opening lines suggest the sleeplessness that will dominate the rejected Heathcliff:

> My slumbers – if I slumber – are not sleep,
> But a continuance of enduring thought,
> Which then I can resist not: in my heart
> There is a vigil, and these eyes but close
> To look within;
>   ('Manfred' Act I, scene I, 3–7)

In response to Catherine's taunt that Heathcliff will forget her when she is dead, he replies in anguish:

Do you reflect that all those words will be branded in my memory, and eating deeper eternally, after you have left me? You know you lie to say I have killed you; and, Catherine, you know that I could as soon forget you, as my existence! Is it not sufficient for your infernal selfishness, that while you are at peace I shall writhe in the torments of hell? (p. 159)

The terrible curse upon Manfred is that he is condemned to live on after his beloved Astarte has died

> There is a power upon me which withholds,
> And makes it my fatality to live –
> If it be life to wear within myself
> This barrenness of spirit, and to be
> My own soul's sepulchre
> (Act I, scene II, 23–7)

This figure of enduring life wracked by grief for the unattainable will be

> Grey-haired with anguish, like these blasted pines,
> Wrecks of a single winter, barkless, branchless,
> A blighted trunk upon a cursed root
> (Act I, scene II, 65–7)

Heathcliff's curse will also be felt as he lives on after Catherine's death:

> So much the worse for me that I am strong. Do I want to live? What kind of living will it be when you – oh God! would *you* like to live with your soul in the grave? (p. 161)

Like Heathcliff's passionate identification with his almost-sister Catherine, Manfred talks of Astarte:

> She was like me in lineaments – her eyes,
> Her hair, her features, all, to the very tone
> Even of her voice, they said were like to mine;
> But soften'd all, and temper'd into beauty;
> She had the same lone thoughts and wanderings
> (Act II, scene II, 105–9)

When the ghost of the long-dead Astarte appears at the request of Nemesis, Manfred comments upon her still living quality:

> Can this be death? there's bloom upon her cheek;
> But now I see it is no living hue,
> But a strange hectic – like the unnatural red
> Which Autumn plants upon the perish'd leaf.
> It is the same! Oh, God! that I should dread
> To look upon the same – Astarte! – No,
> I cannot speak to her – but bid her speak –
> Forgive me or condemn me.
>
> (Act II, scene IV, 98–105)

This bears comparison with the moment when Heathcliff opens up the grave of the long-dead Catherine and comments upon her features still being 'hers yet': there is a feeling that the gap between life and death seems for a moment almost something that could be bridged. Manfred gazes on his beloved and is reminded that

> Thou lovedst me
> Too much, as I loved thee: we were not made
> To torture thus each other, though it were
> The deadliest sin to love as we have loved.
>
> (Act II, scene IV, 120–3)

The threatening posture of the Byronic demon makes a vivid appearance as the outlaw Douglas in Emily's poem 'And now the housedog stretched once more' written on 12 July 1839. Here, a mysterious arrival at a shepherd's door clearly foreshadows Heathcliff's intrusion into the Earnshaw household:

> He'd no refinement to unlearn
> A silence settled on the room
> The cheerful welcome sank to gloom

But not those words though cold and high
So froze their hospitable joy
No – there was something in his face
Some nameless thing they could not trace
And something in his voices tone
Which turned their blood as chill as stone
The ringlets of his long black hair
Fell o'er a cheek most ghastly fair
Youthful he seemed – but worn as they
Who spend too soon their youthful day
When his glance drooped 'twas hard to quell
Unbidden feelings sudden swell
And pity scarce her tears could hide
So sweet that brow with all its pride
But when upraised his eye would dart
An icey shudder through the heart
Compassion changed to horror then
And fear to meet that gaze again.

In *Form and Function in the Novel*, Dorothy Van Ghent refers to Heathcliff's 'anthropomorphized primitive energy, concentrated in activity, terrible in effect':

Emily Brontë insists on Heathcliff's gypsy lack of origins, his lack of orientation and determination in the social world, his equivocal status on the edge of the human. (Van Ghent p. 154)

She points out that the intruding child is referred to as 'it' 21 times before being christened Heathcliff after a dead son of the Earnshaws. The bringer of the gift into the household, Mr. Earnshaw, refers to the orphaned child as being 'a gift from God; though it's as dark almost as if it came from the devil'. This sentiment is echoed by Joseph as he looks at Heathcliff's corpse and says 'Th' divil's harried off his soul.' The visitor's eyes in the Douglas poem have the demonic power of Heathcliff and are seen at the end of the fragment to have 'their basilisk charm':

> But when upraised his eye would dart
> An icy shudder through the heart.
> Compassion changed to horror then
> And fear to meet that gaze again.
> It was not hatred's tiger-glare,
> Nor the wild anguish of despair;
> It was not useless misery
> Which mocks at friendship's sympathy.
> No – lightening all unearthly shone
> Deep in that dark eye's circling zone,
> Such withering lightening as we deem
> None but a spectre's look may beam;
> And glad they were when he turned away
> And wrapt him in his mantle grey,
> Leant down his head upon his arm
> And veiled from view their basilisk charm.

Isabella Linton had eloped with Heathcliff because she had been deluded enough to picture him as 'a hero or romance' whose charms swept away her judgement, while in her letter to Nellie, sent after her arrival at Wuthering Heights, she refers to him as 'a venomous serpent'.

ROLE OF NARRATORS

Edward Chitham argues interestingly that the role of Nelly was introduced into the novel after the narrative had begun and that her central position as a chorus figure grew throughout the revision process. Chitham's argument centres around the role of the dramatic in the novel and the importance of Emily Brontë's reading of Horace's *Ars Poetica*:

> It must never be forgotten that the Brontës' imaginative explorations began with Drama, and as late as 1845 on the journey to York Emily and Anne acted parts as they

journeyed along. They *were* the parts they played, said Emily. From the toy soldiers and Mr Brontë's strange early stratagem to this expedition of grown women, Brontë voices spoke through masks like the masks in Greek tragedy. Emily, taciturn in front of strangers, writes her poetry in metaphorical inverted commas. For all the pages of Brontë small print, written descriptions are not Emily's forte: most of her work, and almost all of *Wuthering Heights*, can be heard or seen. Horace's emphasis on Drama can be seen as a second way in which his interests coincide with those of Emily Brontë. (Chitham p. 29)

The reference made here to the 'strange early stratagem' relates to an incident recalled by Mrs Gaskell as she quotes from Patrick Brontë:

A circumstance now occurs to my mind which I may as well mention. When my children were very young, when, as far as I can remember, the oldest was about ten years of age, and the youngest about four, thinking that they knew more than I had yet discovered, in order to make them speak with less timidity, I deemed that if they were put under a sort of cover I might gain my end; and happening to have a mask in the house, I told them all to stand and speak boldly from under cover of the mask. (Gaskell p. 41)

Chitham quotes Horace's view of the chorus in *Ars Poetica*:

The chorus should maintain his identity as an actor and his active role. He should not interpose material between the acts which is irrelevant to the main theme, and is not inherently appropriate. He should support the worthy and give them friendly advice, control the angry and favour those who are loth to do wrong. He should approve feasts involving a modest table, wholesome justice and legality and the peace that allows city gates to be open;

he should be discreet about matters entrusted to him and beg and pray to the gods that fortune should return to the underprivileged and depart from the overconfident. (*Ars Poetica* 193–201)

Chitham proceeds to suggest that the role of Nelly is perhaps moulded on this pattern. Juliet Barker also suggests that Emily's imaginative writing is externalized in this manner and dramatically presented:

Like her older sister, Emily externalised her imagination; her poems and stories did not seem to her to inhabit her head but were played out before her as if they were creations independent of her control. She was simply a passive spectator who could visualize so strongly that she only wrote what she actually saw. (Barker p. 482)

It is as though Emily created characters who talked as if in a play, which placed a distance between their views and the opinions of the author. This style is also emphasized in the way the Gondal poems were not written in order of Gondal date:

Like *Wuthering Heights* the Gondal narrative ranges over time now forwards, now back, just as in *The Aeneid* there are flashbacks and forward leaps. In other words, epic arrangement is not linear, adhering to the reality of human consciousness in recalling and forecasting time rather than dealing with it in linear mode'. (Chitham p. 68)

As with a dramatic presentation, Emily Brontë is 'conscious of local time and yet willing to annul time in imagination and memory' and 'events happen to people because of who they are, making narrative an unpredictable consideration':

This is entirely consistent with what we have seen in the poems: static or timeless impressions are the root of Emily

Brontë's imagining, and she sees in her mind's eye events happen to the characters, which her rational mind then has to shape into a story. (Chitham p. 71)

STUDY QUESTIONS

1. Both Nellie and Lockwood are narrators of the story in *Wuthering Heights*. Compare the similarities and differences in the way the two tell their tales.
2. Read Byron's poem 'Manfred' and compare the character of the hero there with that of Heathcliff.
3. Read the poems written by Emily Bronte during her time at Law Hill, which you will find in Janet Gezari's *The Complete Poems* (Penguin). Trace the comparisons between them and the descriptive moods in *Wuthering Heights*.

CHAPTER 3

READING *WUTHERING HEIGHTS*

PASSAGE 1 (SUPERNATURAL)

This time, I remembered I was lying in the oak closet, and I heard distinctly the gusty wind, and the driving of the snow; I heard, also, the fir-bough repeat its teasing sound, and ascribed it to the right cause: but, it annoyed me so much, that I resolved to silence it, if possible; and, I thought, I rose and endeavoured to unhasp the casement. The hook was soldered into the staple, a circumstance observed by me, when awake, but forgotten.

'I must stop it, nevertheless!' I muttered, knocking my knuckles through the glass, and stretching an arm out to seize the importunate branch: instead of which, my fingers closed on the fingers of a little, ice-cold hand!

The intense horror of nightmare came over me; I tried to draw back my arm, but, the hand clung to it, and a most melancholy voice sobbed,

'Let me in – let me in!'

'Who are you?' I asked, struggling, meanwhile, to disengage myself.

'Catherine Linton,' it replied, shiveringly (why did I think of *Linton*? I had read *Earnshaw* twenty times for Linton). 'I'm come home, I'd lost my way on the moor!'

As it spoke, I discerned, obscurely, a child's face looking through the window – Terror made me cruel; and, finding it useless to attempt shaking the creature off, I pulled its wrist on to the broken pane, and rubbed it to and fro till the blood ran down and soaked the bed-clothes: still it wailed, 'Let me in!' and maintained its tenacious gripe, almost maddening me with fear.

'How can I?' I said at length. 'Let *me* go, if you want me to let you in!'

The fingers relaxed, I snatched mine through the hole, hurriedly piled the books up in a pyramid against it, and stopped my ears to exclude the lamentable prayer.

I seemed to keep them closed above a quarter of an hour, yet, the instant I listened again, there was the doleful cry moaning on!

'Begone!' I shouted, 'I'll never let you in, not if you beg for twenty years!'

'It's twenty years,' mourned the voice, 'twenty years, I've been a waif for twenty years!'

Thereat began a feeble scratching outside, and the pile of books moved as if thrust forward.

I tried to jump up; but, could not stir a limb; and so yelled aloud, in a frenzy of fright. (p. 25–6)

In an unsigned review published on 15 January 1848 in *Douglas Jerrold's Weekly Newspaper*, the reviewer refers to readers being 'shocked, disgusted, almost sickened by details of cruelty, inhumanity, and the most diabolical hate and vengeance'. Lockwood's dream while imprisoned in the coffin-like oak closet where he is compelled to spend the night after failing to make his escape from the Heights is shockingly vivid with an intensity that is emphasized by it's being the wrist of a child that is dragged 'to and fro' on the broken glass of the window pane. In *The Birth of Wuthering Heights*, Edward Chitham suggests that 'this episode of a dream of a lost child derives from Emily's experience in spring 1845 of the heartache of 20 years' separation from her elder sister, Maria? The "twenty years" of the child's answer, the fact that this is a child not an adult, and therefore not the ghost at the time of her separation from Heathcliff (when she bears a child herself as a married woman), suggests that Emily's vision *started* with the frozen child.' The death of Maria Brontë had taken place 20 years before the writing of this chapter of the novel and the ghostly figure trying to return has an emotional importance for the writer, which far outweighs the seemingly anomalous aspects of the time scheme within a novel which, after all, is so precise about chronological accuracy.

The context of this nightmare is important, and it is worth remembering that Lockwood is compelled to remain at the Heights as a guest since he cannot find his own way back to the Grange on account of the snowstorm, and there is no one there to act as a guide for him. The sense of being imprisoned is highlighted by the way he 'endeavoured' to open the casement window before realizing that the hook 'was soldered into the staple'. The only way out now is by breaking the glass, but it is this very action that leads to the intensity of horror as he grasps hold of a child's 'ice-cold hand'. To fully realize the horror of the nightmare, it has to be remembered that the 'child' is in the air one storey up since Lockwood had already climbed the stairs to reach this bedroom. The description of the lacerating of the child's wrist is made acutely violent through the use of the word 'rubbed' with its connotations of deliberate and repetitive action, and Lockwood's unquestionable complicity in the brutality of the scene is further emphasized by the movement of time. Although the quantity of blood spilled is so evident with the use of the word 'soaked', the child continues to wail and refuses to release his hand as though it is seeking assistance, rescue from falling through the air. The next moment of cruelty is emphasized by Lockwood's deceit as he pretends to offer help before abandoning the child. The question 'How can I?' refers to the enquiry as to how the man holding out his hand and seemingly offering a lifeline to the outsider can effect the help needed. 'Let *me* go, if you want me to let you in!' suggests that he is prepared to allow the child a way in through the window and the evidence that his deceit works is given by the trusting manner in which 'The fingers relaxed'. No sooner does he feel himself released from being required to hold the child's hand than he snatches his own through the hole and 'hurriedly piled the books up in a pyramid against it'. The image of the pyramid suggests the enormous stone mountain he is prepared to put between himself and the 'lamentable prayer' outside. The fact that this pyramid is made of books is appropriate as the urban gentleman attempts to block out the supernatural invasion from outside by relying upon the rational world of literary communication. The importance that books hold for Lockwood is emphasized by him when he visits the Heights towards the end of the novel in order to deliver a written message from Ellen to the younger Catherine. Like her mother, the young girl would have made use of any scrap of paper to write a note:

'You must tell her,' she continued, 'that I would answer her letter, but I have no materials for writing, not even a book from which I might tear a leaf.' (p. 298)

Lockwood's response is one of astonishment as he asks her how she contrives to live in the Heights without them:

'Though provided with a large library, I'm frequently very dull at the Grange – take my books away, and I should be desperate!' (ibid.)

That word 'desperate' contains an echo of his frantic attempt to prevent the ghostly waif from gaining entrance to the Heights.

In her essay on the novel, published in *The English Novel: Form and Function*, Dorothy Van Ghent describes Lockwood as 'the well-mannered urbanite' whose 'antecedents and psychology are so insipid that we care little about them':

Psychologically, Lockwood's dream has only the most perfunctory determinations, and nothing at all of result for the dreamer himself, except to put him uncomfortably out of bed.

READING *WUTHERING HEIGHTS*

However, it is worth recalling Lockwood's own estimation of his character, which he presents to us in the first chapter of the novel when he 'was thrown into the company of a most fascinating creature, a real goddess, in my eyes, as long as she took no notice of me'. Here is the man who looks at life through the glass but has no wish to let anyone in! When the young lady 'understood me, at last, and looked a return – the sweetest of all imaginable looks', Lockwood 'shrunk icily into myself, like a snail, at every glance retired colder and farther' until 'the poor innocent was led to doubt her own senses, and, overwhelmed with confusion at her supposed mistake, persuaded her mamma to decamp'. Lockwood's self-analysis after this earlier moment of deceit was to conclude that he had 'gained the reputation of deliberate heartlessness' but goes on to preen himself with the comment 'how undeserved, I alone can appreciate'.

The language used here refers, of course, to the world of courtship and flirtation and this may initially seem to be a long way from the blood-soaked bedclothes of Lockwood's coffin-like bed. However, there is something infectious about the bleak isolation of the Heights themselves, which acts as a direct contrast to any romantic vision of what it might appear to be like from outside, and this contrast between the world inside the window and outside is brought home to the reader later on in the novel when Isabella describes to Ellen her arrival at her marital home:

> How did you contrive to preserve the common sympathies of human nature when you resided here? I cannot recognise nay sentiment which those around share with me. (p. 134)

Emily Brontë's reading of Sir Walter Scott's *Rob Roy* will have acquainted her with this effect that buildings can have upon personalities, and both Wuthering Heights and Osbaldistone Hall seem to have the power to change the behaviour of those who reside in them, exaggerating traits which already existed within the character and perverting them by making them more extreme. You will find this idea looked at in greater detail in Chapter 2 where there are specific comparisons made between Scott's novel and *Wuthering Heights*.

Lockwood's description of the room and bed to which he has been shown by Zillah is precise and suggests a world cut off from the surroundings:

> The whole furniture consisted of a chair, a clothes-press, and a large oak case, with squares cut out near the top, resembling coach windows.

The last image brings to mind that residence within this self-contained unit may well involve travel to some other place. Lockwood slides back the panels before getting in and pulling them together again and these moveable panels foreshadow the coffin in which Catherine Earnshaw/Linton is laid, which can be removed at one side to allow for the corpse of Heathcliff to be slid in. When Lockwood's cry brings Heathcliff into the room, the urbane southerner refers to the place as 'swarming with ghosts and goblins' and to the ghostly child as 'the little fiend' who 'probably would have strangled me'. This supernatural aspect of the Heights is endorsed later when Heathcliff's corpse is discovered in the same bed.

For an example of the effect of dismal surroundings upon an urbane Londoner, it is worth turning to Samuel Johnson's *Journey to the Western Isles*:

> We were in this place at ease and by choice, and had no evils to suffer or to fear; yet the imaginations excited by the view of an unknown and untravelled wilderness are not such as arise in the artificial solitude of parks and gardens, a flattering notion of self-sufficiency, a placid indulgence of voluntary delusions, a secure expansion of the fancy, or a cool concentration of the mental powers.

The phantoms which haunt a desert are want and misery, and danger; the evils of dereliction rush upon the thoughts; man is made unwillingly acquainted with his own weakness, and meditation hews him only how little he can sustain, and how little he can perform. p. 686–7.

As if to emphasize the way in which the room within a room, the coffin-like bed to which he had been shown, belongs to a different time scheme altogether, Lockwood concludes with words that are reminiscent of Macbeth's state of mind after the murder of Banquo and the appearance of the dead man's ghost. In the Shakespeare play, Macbeth asks Lady Macbeth 'what is the night?' and receives the reply 'Almost at odds with morning, which is which' (*Macbeth* Act III, scene IV, 125–6). Here, a weary Lockwood says:

Not three o'clock, yet! I could have taken oath it had been six – time stagnates here. (p. 28)

PASSAGE 2 (CHILDHOOD)

Certainly, she had ways with her such as I never saw a child take up before; and she put all of us past our patience fifty times and oftener in a day: from the hour she came down stairs, till the hour she went to bed, we had not a minute's security that she wouldn't be in mischief. Her spirits were always at high-water mark, her tongue always going – singing, laughing, and plaguing everybody who would not do the same. A wild, wick slip she was – but, she had the bonniest eye, and sweetest smile, and lightest foot in the parish; and, after all, I believe she meant no harm; for when once she made you cry in good earnest, it seldom happened that she would not keep you company, and oblige you to be quiet that you might comfort her.

She was much too fond of Heathcliff. The greatest punishment we could invent for her was to keep her separate from him: yet, she got chided more than any of us on his account.

39

In play, she liked, exceedingly, to act the little mistress; using her hands freely, and commanding her companions: she did so to me, but I would not bear slapping, and ordering; and so I let her know.

Now, Mr Earnshaw did not understand jokes from his children: he had always been strict and grave with them; and Catherine, on her part, had no idea why her father should be crosser and less patient in his ailing condition, than he was in his prime.

His peevish reproofs wakened in her a naughty delight to provoke him; she was never so happy as when we were all scolding her at once, and she defying us with her bold, saucy look, and her ready words; turning Joseph's religious curses into ridicule, baiting me, and doing just what her father hated most, showing how her pretended insolence, which he though teal, had more power over Heathcliff than his kindness: how the boy would do her bidding in anything, and his only when it suited his own inclination.

After behaving as badly as possible all day, she sometimes came fondling to make it up at night.

'Nay, Cathy,' the old man would say, 'I cannot love thee; thou'rt worse than thy brother. Go, say thy prayers, child, and ask God's pardon. I doubt thy mother and I must rue that we ever reared thee!'

That made her cry, at first; and then, being repulsed continually hardened her, and she laughed if I told her to say she was sorry for her faults, and beg to be forgiven. (p. 42–3)

In a letter to W. S. Williams, 12 May 1848, Charlotte Brontë wrote about the world of teachers and governesses stressing the need to possess an 'innate sympathy' with children:

He or she who possesses this faculty, this sympathy – though perhaps not otherwise highly accomplished – need never fear failure in the career of instruction. Children will be docile with them, will improve under them; parents will consequently repose in them confidence. Their task will be comparatively light, their path comparatively smooth. If the faculty be absent, the life of a teacher will be a struggle from beginning to end. (*The Brontës* p. 212–13)

When Mr. Earnshaw set out for Liverpool, he promised to return with gifts for his children, and it is with some significance that Catherine chose a whip: her dominant character will be developed throughout the early stages of the novel. However, when he returns with 'a dirty, ragged, black-haired child', the initial family reactions to the newcomer are hostile. When Catherine understands that her father has lost the whip he was bringing for her, she takes the loss out on the child guest by 'grinning and spitting at the stupid little thing'. Nevertheless, within a few days, she and Heathcliff are 'very thick', and we see the quick and changeable character that Catherine reveals throughout the novel. The 'wild, wick slip' referred to in the passage has a quality of living vitality that does not harbour grudges but works instead by impulsive movement. It is significant, by contrast, that when the children suffer from measles, both 'Cathy and her brother harassed' Nelly 'terribly' while Heathcliff 'was as uncomplaining as a lamb'. This image used by Nelly, however, does not convey much sense of innocence since it was 'hardness, not gentleness' which made him 'give little trouble'. The contrast between the children, spontaneity as opposed to brooding, is developed in the novel as Catherine becomes the person who can say 'I did nothing deliberately' having pinched Nelly, shaken Hareton and slapped Edgar round the face all in the space of some few moments. As Nelly tells it, 'She never had power to conceal her passion, it always set her whole complexion in a blaze' (p. 70). In direct contrast to this, Heathcliff's language expresses the teenager's concern for revenge in a calculating and quiet manner as he sits by the fire on Christmas night:

He leant his two elbows on his knees, and his chin on his hands, and remained wrapt in dumb meditation. On

my enquiring the subject of his thoughts, he answered
gravely –
   'I'm trying to settle how I shall pay Hindley back. I
don't care how long I wait, if I can only do it, at last. I
hope he will not die before I do!'
   'For shame, Heathcliff!' said I. 'It is for God to punish
wicked people; we should learn to forgive.'
   'No, God won't have the satisfaction that I shall,' he
returned. 'I only wish I knew the best way! Let me alone,
and I'll plan it out: while I'm thinking of that, I don't feel
pain.' (p. 60)

The 'mischief', 'singing', 'laughing' and 'plaguing everybody' referred to in Passage 2 has an immediacy and spontaneity that is sharply different from this other portrait of
childhood with the brooding figure who plots harm to
others.
   When Nelly refers to Catherine's spirits as 'always at high-
water mark' and as having 'the bonniest eye, and sweetest
smile, and lightest foot in the parish', she presents Lockwood
with the picture of a child brimming with health and vitality. In her essay, 'A Fresh Approach to Wuthering Heights',
Q. D. Leavis includes a reference to Catherine Sinclair's 1839
novel *Holiday House* where the author provided a preface
emphasizing precisely this sort of childish vitality:

   In these pages the author has endeavoured to paint that
   species of noisy, frolicsome, mischievous children, now
   almost extinct, wishing to preserve a sort of fabulous
   remembrance of days long past, when young people were
   like wild horses on the prairies, rather than like well-bro-
   ken hacks on the road.

However, as a precursor to that later moment when the
image of the cat and the wounded bird is presented where
the bird's injuries are seen as a bait (cf. comment on

Passage 4), Nelly perhaps unwittingly reveals how self-centred this child is. When she has made you cry 'in good earnest', she behaves in such a manner as to require **you** to comfort **her**. It is perhaps this image of pretence, acting as the wounded bird, which prompts Catherine to refer to lapwings in her semi-delirious scene with Nelly:

> 'Bonny bird; wheeling over our heads in the middle of the moor. It wanted to get to its nest, for the clouds touched the swells, and it felt rain coming. This feather was picked up from the heath, the bird was not shot – we saw its nest in the winter, full of little skeletons. Heathcliff set a trap over it, and the old ones dare not come. I made him promise he'd never shoot a lapwing, after that, and he didn't. (p. 121)

The cruelty which children can show towards animals is echoed in Anne Brontë's *Agnes Grey*, being written at the same time as *Wuthering Heights*, as the eponymous governess talks with her child-pupil, Tom, about his attitude towards birds after having found him with a trap:

> 'Why do you catch them?'
> 'Papa says they do harm.'
> 'And what do you do with them, when you catch them?'
> 'Different things. Sometimes I give them to the cat; sometimes I cut them in pieces with my penknife; but the next, I mean to roast alive.' (p. 78)

Anne Brontë's novel presents a picture of childhood which reveals significant parallels with *Wuthering Heights*. The governess finds one of her charges, Fanny, to be 'a mischievous, intractable little creature' whose favourite weapon is 'spitting in the faces of those who incurred her displeasure' (*Agnes Grey* p. 90). When Agnes cannot control the three children she is employed to look after and educate, they escape outside in a manner reminiscent of Cathy and Heathcliff whose 'chief amusements' were 'to run away to the moors in the morning and remain there all day' (p. 46):

> All three escaped me, and ran out of the house into the garden, where they plunged about in the snow, shouting and screaming in exultant glee.
>
> What must I do? If I followed them, I should probably be unable to capture one, and only drive them farther away; if I did not, how was I to get them in? and what would their parents think of me, if they saw or heard the children rioting, hatless, bonnetless, gloveless, and bootless, in the deep, soft snow? (*Agnes Grey* p. 94–5)

Nelly shares some of Agnes's difficulties as a governess, and she comments about not 'daring to speak a syllable for fear of losing the small power I still retained over the unfriended creatures' (p. 47) as she watches them 'growing more reckless daily'.

The picture we have of Catherine in the passage combines that spontaneity referred to along with a wilfulness that denotes the child who wishes to be in charge of her world. When 'in play', she likes to 'act the little mistress': we can see precisely why the choice of a whip as a gift from her father was particularly appropriate. She is seen as 'commanding her companions', and here she seems to include Nelly herself, while at the same time to be supremely unaware of the difficulties facing her father. She is unsympathetic about his 'ailing condition' and takes a delight in provoking him and 'doing just what her father hated most'. At the end of a day of mischief, she 'came fondling to make it up at night' where the verb is suggestive again of a cat-like movement that seems to have no memory of her past behaviour and little sense of culpability. Her tears at being repulsed by the single parent who suggests that 'thy mother and I must rue that we ever reared thee' are soon replaced by a hardening of her character and by scornful laughter.

With the death of Mr. Earnshaw, we are presented with a picture of how Catherine and Heathcliff, two orphaned children, seek solace with each other:

> The little souls were comforting each other with better thoughts than I could have hit on; no parson in the world ever pictured Heaven so beautifully as they did, in their innocent talk; and, while I sobbed, and listened, I could not help wishing we were all there safe together. (p. 44)

This image of the vulnerable children coming to terms with death echoes Emily Brontë's poem dated 19 December 1841 from the Gondal notebook where Angelica, the daughter of Lord Alfred S. of Aspin Castle, seeks comfort with Gerald who is her half brother:

> I do not weep, I would not weep;
> Our Mother needs no tears:
> Dry thine eyes too, 'tis vain to keep
> This causeless grief for years
>
> What though her brow be changed and cold,
> Her sweet eyes closed for ever?
> What though the stone – the darksome mould
> Our mortal bodies sever?
>
> What though her hand smooth ne'er again
> Those silken locks of thine –
> Nor through long hours of future pain
> Her kind face o'er thee shine?
>
> Remember still she is not dead
> She sees us Gerald now
> Laid where her angel spirit fled
> 'Mid heath and frozen snow
>
> And from that world of heavenly light
> Will she not always bend
> To guide us in our lifetime's night
> And guard us to the end?

Thou know'st she will, and well may'st mourn
That we are left below
But not that she can ne'er return
To share our earthly woe –

This sense of the inseparable nature of the two children emphasized by Nelly's words and the mutual comfort they take from each other's company strike a reminiscent chord with Mrs. Gaskell's account of the reaction of the Brontë children to the situation where their mother was dying:

> ...the six little creatures used to walk out, hand in hand, towards the glorious wild moors, which in after days they loved so passionately; the elder ones taking thoughtful care for the toddling wee things. (Gaskell p. 37)

This close-knit sense of Catherine and Heathcliff's shared loss makes her betrayal of him later only more acute.

PASSAGE 3 (WINDOWS)

'Don't you cant, Nelly,' he said. 'Nonsense! We ran from the top of the Heights to the park, without stopping – Catherine completely beaten in the race, because she was barefoot. You'll have to seek for her shoes in the bog to-morrow. We crept through a broken hedge, groped our way up the path, and planted ourselves on a flower-pot under the drawing-room window. The light came from thence; they had not put up the shutters, and the curtains were only half closed. Both of us were able to look in by standing on the basement, and clinging to the ledge, and we saw – ah! it was beautiful – a splendid place carpeted with crimson, and crimson-covered chairs and tables, and a pure white ceiling bordered by gold, a shower of glass-drops hanging in silver chains from the centre, and shimmering with little soft tapers. Old Mr and Mrs Linton were not there. Edgar and his sister had it entirely to themselves; shouldn't they have been happy? We should have thought ourselves in heaven! And now, guess what your good children were doing? Isabella – I believe she is eleven, a year younger than Cathy – lay screaming at the farther end of the room, shrieking as if witches were running red hot needles into her. Edgar stood on the hearth weeping silently, and in the middle of the table sat a little dog, shaking its paw and yelping, which, from their mutual accusations, we had understood they had nearly pulled in two between them. The idiots! That was their pleasure! to quarrel who should hold a heap of warm hair, and each begin to cry because both, after struggling to get it, refused to take it. We laughed outright at the petted things, we did despise them! When would you catch me wishing to have what Catherine wanted? or find us by ourselves, seeking entertainment in yelling and sobbing, and rolling on the ground, divided by the whole room? I'd not exchange, for a thousand lives, my condition here, for Edgar Linton's at Thrushcross Grange – not if I might have the privilege of flinging Joseph off the highest gable, and painting the house-front with Hindley's blood!' (p. 48)

Emily Brontë's diary paper of 30 July 1841, her twenty-third birthday, is prefixed with two tiny ink sketches she did of herself, one writing by the fire and the other standing looking out of the window, and this image of looking from one world into another threads its way throughout the novel. In his account of the background to the writing of *Wuthering Heights*, Edward Chitham suggests that while none of the diary papers show Emily writing out of doors, she undoubtedly walked out to gain inspiration while 'the gazing out of windows is also part of her 'work' to gain in day-dreams her initial ideas' (Chitham p. 13).

To gaze intently or fixedly is to become rapt up with the object of the gaze, and the two children looking through the windows of the Grange are presented with a world which offers light, refinement and luxury, all of which contrast with the flogging and fasting of the Heights. Escaping from their imprisonment in the wash house, the children 'ramble at liberty' (p. 47) before deciding to 'go and see whether the

Lintons passed their Sunday evenings standing shivering in corners, while their father and mother sat eating and drinking, singing and laughing, and burning their eyes out before the fire'. The exuberance of the escapees is felt with Heathcliff's opening statements about running a race from the top of the Heights to the park 'without stopping'. The children's competitive spark is emphasized by the following comment about Catherine being 'completely beaten in the race', while the careless and self-centred aspect of their adventure is made clear when the servant and surrogate mother, Nelly, is told that she will have to seek for Catherine's shoes 'in the bog to-morrow'. Heathcliff's narrative conveys the spying through the window in a vivid manner as the children 'crept through a broken hedge' before groping their way up the path. The groping movement emphasizes the darkness outside, which will act as a strong contrast with the lights within the Grange, and the narrator leads Nelly to the brink of the gazed-upon wonder with dramatic control:

> Both of us were able to look in by standing on the basement, and clinging to the ledge, and we saw – ah! it was beautiful – a splendid place carpeted with crimson, and crimson-covered chairs and tables, and a pure white ceiling bordered by gold, a shower of glass-drops hanging in silver chains from the centre, and shimmering with little soft tapers.

The interjected 'ah!' allows for a pause before one contemplates the difference between the world inside and the darkness outside. The world of wealth and colour appears tantalizingly inviting with the repetition of 'crimson' and the combination of white, gold and silver. The room presents a vision of a 'pure' landscape far removed from the rugged bleakness of the moors, and the waterfall effect of the 'shower of glass-drops' is stilled into the 'silver chains' which shimmer. However, the seductive danger of the vision is only fully realized once Cathy has been taken inside this new

world which she and Heathcliff have glimpsed and is transformed by it losing her older connection with the world of
the 'heath'.

The sense of social mobility, linked to independent
means, offering a new perspective is evident in Charlotte
Brontë's reaction to Mary Taylor's European tour in 1841,
and she wrote to Ellen Nussey in August 1841 in terms
which present a clear yearning for life on the other side of
the window:

> Mary's letter spoke of some of the pictures & cathedrals
> she had seen – pictures the most exquisite – & cathedrals
> the most venerable – I hardly know what swelled to my
> throat as I read her letter – such a vehement impatience
> of restraint & steady work. such a strong wish for wings –
> wings such as wealth can furnish – such an urgent thirst
> to see – to know to learn – something internal seemed
> to expand boldly for a minute. I was tantalized with the
> consciousness of faculties unexercised – then all collapsed
> and I despaired (*The Brontës* p. 240).

However, the way towards social mobility is clearly linked to
wealth, and it is no surprise therefore that when Cathy talks
to Ellen about the reasons for marrying Edgar, the social
aspects/wealth are uppermost in her decision making. She
says that Edgar 'will be rich, and I shall like to be the greatest woman of the neighbourhood' (p. 78). She is also aware
that this desire is to do only with the present and that she is
betraying her heart by engineering this social
advancement:

> I was only going to say that heaven did not seem to be
> my home; and I broke my heart with weeping to come
> back to earth; and the angels were so angry that they
> flung me out, into the middle of the heath on the top of
> Wuthering Heights; where I woke sobbing for joy. That
> will do to explain my secret, as well as the other. I've no

more business to marry Edgar Linton than I have to be in heaven; and if the wicked man in there had not brought Heathcliff so low, I shouldn't have thought of it. It would degrade me to marry Heathcliff, now; so he shall never know how I love him; and that, not because he's handsome, Nelly, but because he's more myself than I am. Whatever our souls are made of, his and mine are the same, and Linton's is as different as a moonbeam from lightening, or frost from fire. (p. 80)

The images here echo the 'pure white', the glass and the 'silver' from inside the Grange as the children stared mesmerized through the window to glimpse the so-called Heaven of wealth and social standing.

In her sustained analysis of looking through the window from one world to another, Dorothy Van Ghent makes it clear that the seductive power of the vision only affects Catherine:

Here the two unregenerate waifs look in from the night on the heavenly vision of the refinements and securities of the most privileged human estate. But Heathcliff rejects the vision: seeing the Linton children blubbering and bored there (*they* cannot get *out!*), he senses the menace of its limitations; while Catherine is fatally tempted. She is taken in by the Lintons, and now it is Heathcliff alone outside looking through the window. (Van Ghent 161)

Heathcliff recognizes with a degree of scorn that the world of violence, which has surrounded him since his arrival as an orphan outcast at the Heights, is just as much a part of this life within the lighted and wealthy Grange. The two children inside are spending their time teasing a little dog which is now 'shaking its paw and yelping' having been 'nearly pulled in two between them'. Isabella's own springer,

Fanny, was later discovered 'suspended to a handkerchief, and nearly at its last gasp' (p. 128) when she eloped with Heathcliff, and his comment on this echoes that scornful note of recognition which exposed the hypocrisy of the children in the Grange:

> The first thing she saw me do, on coming out of the Grange, was to hang up her little dog, and when she pleaded for it, the first words I uttered were a wish that I had the hanging of every being belonging to her, except one: possibly, she took that exception for herself – But no brutality disgusted her – I suppose she has an innate admiration of it, if only her precious person were secure from injury! (p. 149)

Catherine is trapped by the charms of this shimmering world inside the Grange without recognizing the nature of imprisonment in what Heathcliff describes as 'silver chains' and only later on does she desperately want to return to the openness of the earlier landscapes. In Chapter 12, having secured the man and the social standing his wealth brings, she lies in bed in the Grange semi-delirious and desperately wanting the window open:

> 'Oh, if I were but in my own bed in the old house!' she went on bitterly, wringing her hands. 'And that wind sounding in the firs by the lattice. Do let me feel it – it comes straight down the moor – do let me have one breath!' (p. 123)

Ellen attempts to pacify her by holding the window open for a moment, and a 'cold blast rushed through' as if to emphasize the impossibility of ever returning. Undeterred by the unwelcoming experience of this, she tells Ellen that she is sure that she could be herself again 'were I once among the heather on those hills' and asks her to open the window again 'wide'. When Ellen's pragmatic nature makes her reply that the open window will give the invalid 'your death of cold', Catherine answers from within that shimmering silver and gold prison of the Grange:

'You won't give me a chance of life, you mean.' (p. 125)

Crossing the room, she throws opens the window herself to embrace a mixture of both life and death:

And sliding from the bed before I could hinder her, she crossed the room, walking very uncertainly, threw it back, and bent out, careless of the frosty air that cut about her shoulders as keen as a knife. (ibid.)

In the distance, she imagines that she can see the lights of the Heights 'shining' and, in her delirium, calls across the moors to Heathcliff who had remained outside that seductive crimson, gold and silver.

The image of looking for a better world on the other side of the glass is a striking image in Charlotte's novel, *The Professor*, on which she was working at the same time as Emily was writing *Wuthering Heights*. As Juliet Barker notes in *The Brontës*, 'Returning to the habits of their childhood, the sisters wrote their books in close collaboration, reading passages aloud to each other and discussing the handling of their plots and their characters as they walked round and round the dining-room table each evening' (Barker p. 500). In the Brussels school, William Crimsworth gazes in his mind through the 'fenêtre fermée' hoping to find 'some chink or crevice' through which he might 'get a peep at the consecrated ground' of the neighbouring 'pensionnat de demoiselles':

Not only then, but many a time after, especially in moments of weariness and low spirits, did I look with dissatisfied eyes on that most tantalizing board, longing to tear it away and get a glimpse of the green region which I imagined to lie beyond. (*The Professor* p. 96)

Charlotte's image continues with a direct echo of the dream sequence at the opening of *Wuthering Heights* referred to in Passage 1:

> I knew a tree grew close up to the window, for though there were as yet no leaves to rustle, I often heard at night the tapping of branches against the panes.

As the passage continues, the 'unseen paradise' has a direct counterpart to the children's view of the inside of the Grange:

> In the daytime, when I listened attentively, I could hear, even through the boards, the voices of the demoiselles in their hours of recreation, and, to speak the honest truth, my sentimental reflections were occasionally a trifle disarranged by the not quite silvery, in fact the too often brazen sounds, which, rising from the unseen paradise below, penetrated clamorously into my solitude. (ibid.)

The Pensionnat where Charlotte was so happy was in fact like a prison to Emily as Katherine Frank's account makes clear in *Emily Brontë: A Chainless Soul*:

> The Pensionnat garden – even on the chilly February day when the Brontes first saw it – was the inner sancrum of the school. Surrounded on all four sides by other houses, it was entirely cut off, like a fortress, from the din and dirt and noisy humanity of city life... For Emily all the carefully cultivated rose bushes and artfully pruned hedges in the world could not conceal the fact that the Pensionnat garden was – in addition to being a playground, open-air classroom and retreat – a prison. A prison within a prison. (Frank 160–1)

After gazing through the window of the Grange, Catherine becomes virtually imprisoned there by her illness occasioned by having been caught by the guard dog, but it is this captivity which seduces her from her previous freedom of spirit and replaces her natural exuberant childhood with social concerns for status, which will contribute towards her rejection of Heathcliff.

PASSAGE 4 (VIOLENCE)

'"He's there...is he?" exclaimed my companion, rushing to the gap. "If I can get my arm out I can hit him!"

'I'm afraid, Ellen, you'll set me down as really wicked – but you don't know all, so don't judge! I wouldn't have aided or abetted an attempt on even *his* life, for anything – Wish that he were dead, I must; and therefore, I was fearfully disappointed, and unnerved by terror for the consequences of my taunting speech, when he flung himself on Earnshaw's weapon and wrenched it from his grasp.

'The charge exploded, and the knife, in springing back, closed into its owner's wrist. Heathcliff pulled it away by main force, slitting up the flesh as it passed on, and thrust it dripping into his pocket. He then took a stone, struck down the division between two windows and sprung in. his adversary had fallen senseless with excessive pain, and the flow of blood that gushed from an artery, or a large vein.

'The ruffian kicked and trampled on him, and dashed his head repeatedly against the flags; holding me with one hand, meantime, to prevent me summoning Joseph.

'He exerted preter-human self-denial in abstaining from finishing him, completely; but getting out of breath, he finally desisted, and dragged the apparently inanimate body onto the settle.

'There he tore off the sleeve of Earnshaw's coat, and bound up the wound with brutal roughness, spitting and cursing, during the operation, as energetically as he had kicked before.

'Being at liberty, I lost no time in seeking the old servant; who, having gathered by degrees the purport of my hasty tale, hurried below, gasping, as he descended the steps two at once.

' "Whet is thur tuh do, nah? whet is thur tuh do, nah?"

' "There's this to do," thundered Heathcliff, "that your master's mad; and should he last another month, I'll have him to an asylum. And how the devil did you come to fasten me out, you toothless hound? Don't stand muttering and mumbling there. Come, I'm not going to nurse him. Wash that stuff away; and mind the sparks of your candle – it is more than half brandy!"

' "Und soa, yah been murthering on him?" exclaimed Joseph, lifting his hands and eyes in horror. "If iver Aw seed a seeght loike this! May the Lord – "

'Heathcliff gave him a push onto his knees, in the middle of the blood, and flung a towel to him; but instead of proceeding to dry it up, he joined his hands, and began a prayer which excited my laughter from its odd phraseology. I was in condition of mind to be shocked at nothing; in fact, I was as reckless as some malefactors show themselves at the foot of the gallows. (p. 176)

This passage where Hindley attempts to kill Heathcliff but is himself nearly murdered is one of particular graphic brutality. The background to the scene has echoes of the world of Shakespeare's *Macbeth* as Hindley talks of 'Treachery and violence' (p. 175) and refers to the returning Heathcliff, who knocks at the door, 'Damn the hellish villain'. In terms that echo Macbeth's arguments when trying to persuade himself that murder and treachery are 'Bloody instructions which, being taught, return/To plague th'inventor,' Isabella comments that she would

> ... be glad of a retaliation that wouldn't recoil on myself; but treachery, and violence, are spears pointed at both ends – they wound those who resort to them, worse than their enemies. (p. 174)

With the thwarting of Hindley's attempt, the language of the passage is precise in its violence, and the elasticity of the movement of the knife blade 'in springing back' is felt intensely with the phrase 'closed into its owner's wrist'. The finality of the word 'closed' is given particular horror by being followed by 'into', which has considerably greater impact than any alternative such as 'on' or 'in'. When Heathcliff pulls the knife out of Hindley's wrist, the brutal strength of 'by main force' is given particularly violent emphasis by being associated with 'slitting up the flesh' and 'dripping'. The flow of blood that 'gushed' out is again precisely rendered by the reference to 'an artery, or large vein'. As if the wounding itself is not enough, Heathcliff's action in dashing Hindley's head 'repeatedly against the flags' is compounded in violence and intent by the deliberate manner in which he holds Isabella with one hand in order to prevent her summoning assistance, and the pushing of Joseph to his knees 'in the middle of the blood' has again a particular visual quality to it associated with the domestic chore of washing the 'stuff' away with a towel. The echoes here of Lady Macbeth's comment about 'A little water clears us of this deed' are followed by Isabella's almost hysterical laughter at Joseph's association of being on his knees with the normal attribute of prayer. That gruesome connection between extreme violence and laughter is itself an echo of the scene immediately following the murder of Duncan when the drunken porter 'had thought to have let in some of all professions that go the primrose way to th'everlasting bonfire' (*Macbeth* II, iii, 17–18).

As Alexander and Smith point out in *The Oxford Companion to the Brontës*, the family 'knew the works of Shakespeare almost as well as they did the Bible', and this haunting sense of the connection between blood and nightmare, extreme violence and revenge, which is central to the tragedy of *Macbeth*, informs much of the world of *Wuthering Heights*. Heathcliff had already referred to 'painting the house-front with Hindley's blood' where the association between painting and blood echoes Lady Macbeth's comment after the murder of Duncan while he stays overnight in their house:

'Tis the eye of childhood
That fears a painted devil. If he do bleed
I'll gild the faces of the grooms withal,
For it must seem their guilt.

After the murder of his friend Banquo, Macbeth refers to himself as 'The secret'st man of blood', and in her madness, Lady Macbeth cannot escape the nightmare of returning visions of bloodshed as she questions 'who would have thought the old man to have had so much blood in him?' Again, when Catherine is in a state of semi-hallucination in her bedroom, in Chapter 12, she tells Nelly that her 'brain got confused, and I screamed unconsciously', and it is almost as if she felt like Shakespeare's bloody hero, having murdered something of complete value, who dreads 'sleeping, my dreams appal me' echoing the traitor's comment immediately after he has murdered Duncan:

How is't with me when every noise appals me

The brutal physicality of Heathcliff in the passage where he almost kills Hindley also reflects Emily Brontë's reading of one her favourite Scott novels, *Rob Roy*, where the uncompromising violence of Helen Campbell is witnessed as she commands a testimony of Dougal's loyalty by telling him 'to cut out their tongues and put them into each other's throats to try which would there best knap Southron, or to tear out their hearts and put them into each other's breasts to see which would there best plot treason against the MacGregor'. However, to see how much Emily Brontë used her sources in both Scott and Shakespeare for her own distinctly individual effects, one must recognize how the comments of Helen Campbell have a ferocious martial tone to them while the use of those phrases concerning 'painting' and 'house-front' associate the vengeful young Heathcliff with the horrors of domestic murder. This connection between bloody violence and domestic relationships is clearly expressed by the servant in Scott's novel, Andrew Fairservice, when he tells the narrator that he has heard wives berating their husbands with 'sic grewsome wishes, that men should be slaughtered like sheep – and that they should lapper their hands to the elbows in their heart's blude' (*Rob Roy* p. 250) The violence contained in *Rob Roy* culminates in the brutal murder of the cowardly Morris as he is hurled over a cliff edge into a lake and here again the language finds its echoes in *Wuthering Heights*:

> The victim was held fast by some, while others, binding a large heavy stone in a plaid, tied it around his neck, and others again eagerly stripped him of some parts of his dress. Half-naked, and thus manacled, they hurled him into the lake, there about twelve feet deep, drowning his last death-shriek with a loud halloo of vindictive triumph, above which, however, the yell of mortal agony was distinctly heard. (*Rob Roy* p. 267)

In an unsigned review of the novel for Britannia, 15 January 1848, the reviewer highlighted the violence and brutality in the portrayal of Heathcliff:

> *Wuthering Heights* would have been a far better romance if Heathcliff alone had been a being of stormy passions, instead of all the other characters being nearly as violent and destructive as himself. In fiction, too, as the imitation of nature can never be so vivid and exact as in painting, that imitation is insufficient of itself to afford pleasure, and when it deals with brutal subjects it becomes positively disgusting. It is of course impossible to prescribe rules for either the admission or the rejection of what is shocking and dreadful. It is nothing to say that reality

is faithfully followed the aim of fiction is to afford some sensation of delight.

However, the violence expressed by Heathcliff finds its counterpart elsewhere in the novel, and he is by no means alone in expressing himself through cruelty and bloodshed. The extreme violence towards a child, albeit a ghostly one, is the focal point of Passage 1 in this section of the book, and the violent behaviour of the Linton children towards their dog is referred to in comments upon Passage 3. The connection between violence and love is brought home to the reader with precise clarity when young Edgar Linton calls at the Heights to woo Catherine in Volume I, Chapter 8. After Catherine has slapped him round the face in a fit of temper, he marches towards the door with determination, saying 'You've made me afraid, and ashamed of you... I'll not come here again!' However, in an interesting reversal of what one might have expected:

> The soft thing looked askance through the window – he possessed the power to depart, as much as a cat possesses the power to leave a mouse half killed, or a bird half eaten – (p. 71)

In this image, which mixtures playful teasing and cruelty, it is Edgar who is the predator, and the wilful Catherine, who says that she will cry herself sick, is the vulnerable bait. There is more close reference to this scene in Passage 8 (Love). The image of the cruelty of cats was not new to Emily since she had already unsettled her teacher in Brussels, M. Heger, with her essay titled 'Le Chat', in which she recognized their similarity to human beings by virtue of their cruelty, lack of gratitude and hypocritical fawning. The essay concludes with the image of a cat that has a half-devoured rat in its mouth leaving only the tail dangling down from its lips. In 'Le Papillon', translated by Sue Lonoff in *The Belgian Essays: Charlotte Brontë and Emily Brontë*, we are presented with a vision of the overriding violence of the natural world, which precedes Darwin's theories of survival of the fittest:

> All creation is equally mad. Behold those flies playing above the brook; the swallows and fish diminish their number every minute. These will become, in their turn, the prey of some tyrant of the air or water; and man for his amusement or his needs will kill their murderers. Nature is an inexplicable problem; it exists on a principle of destruction. Every being must be the tireless instrument of death to others, or itself must cease to live ...

The image of the cat's violence is associated also with Isabella Linton as she attempts to withdraw her hand from Catherine's grasp in Volume I, Chapter 10. Having become fascinated by Heathcliff and wishing to be in his company, she cannot endure being teased by the 'dog in a manger' Cathy and finding that she cannot get herself out of her sister-in-law's grasp

> she began to make use of her nails, and their sharpness presently ornamented the detainer's with crescents of red (p. 104).

Catherine then refers to Isabella as having a 'vixen face' and being 'a tigress' (p. 105) in possession of 'talons'. Heathcliff's response is characteristically brutal and to the point:

> 'I'd wrench them off her fingers, if they ever menaced me'.

PASSAGE 5 (REVENGE)

'Well,' replied I, 'I hope you'll be kind to the boy, Mr Heathcliff, or you'll not keep him that long, and he's all you have akin in the wide world that you will ever know – remember.'

'I'll be *very* kind to him, you needn't fear!' he said, laughing. 'Only nobody else must be kind to him – I'm jealous of monopolizing his affection – And, to begin my kindness, Joseph! bring the lad some breakfast – Hareton, you infernal calf, begone to your work. Yes, Nell,' he added when they were departed, 'my son is prospective owner of your place, and I should not wish him to die till I was certain of being his successor. Besides, he's *mine*, and I want the triumph of seeing *my* descendent fairly lord of their estates; my child hiring their children, to till their fathers' lands for wages – That is the sole consideration which can make me endure the whelp – I despise him for himself, and hate him for the memories he revives! But, that consideration is sufficient; he's as safe with me, and shall be tended as carefully as your master tends his own – I have a room upstairs, furnished for him in handsome style – I've engaged a tutor, also, to come three times a week, from twenty miles distance, to teach him what he pleases to learn. I've ordered Hareton to obey him: and in fact, I've arranged every thing with a view to preserve the superior and the gentleman in him, above his associates – I do regret, however, that he so little deserves the trouble – if I wished any blessing in the world, it was to find him a worthy object of pride, and I'm bitterly disappointed with the whey-faced whining wretch!'

While he was speaking, Joseph returned, bearing a basin of milk-porridge, and placed it before Linton. He stirred round the homely mess with a look of aversion, and affirmed he could not eat it.

I saw the old man servant shared largely in his master's scorn of the child, though he was compelled to retain the sentiment in his heart, because Heathcliff plainly meant his underlings to hold him in honour. (p. 206)

Heathcliff's appearance as an avaricious man whose financial calculations involve him taking his revenge with considerable care and vindictive malice is highlighted in this passage where, following the death of his mother, the young invalid,

Linton, is brought to live with his father whom he has never seen. Ellen has just brought the 13-year-old boy up to the Heights, and the gloomy entrance of this young instrument of revenge has already been emphasized by Linton's surveying 'the carved front, and low-browed lattices; the straggling gooseberry bushes, and crooked firs' (p. 204). The house itself seems to reflect the physiognomy of its owner, the beetling eyebrows staring out of an immovable face and the malicious ferocity with which the father greets this son whom he has never seen is conveyed like a slap in the face:

> You are my son, then, I'll tell you; and your mother was a wicked slut to leave you in ignorance of the sort of father you possessed. (p. 206)

When Ellen reminds Heathcliff that this boy is 'all you have akin in the wide world that you will ever know,' there seems to be an appeal to the social feelings of Heathcliff who had entered the novel as the orphaned child. Never having known his own parents and his wife whom he had married out of sheer hatred having died he has now only one possibility of close domestic union, and Ellen reminds him of how he should be aware of the fragility of this young boy. However, the mocking sarcasm of Heathcliff's rejoinder gives the reader little hope that Linton will be greeted with any affection, and the italicized '*very*' raises the prospect of the opposite of the word 'kind' which follows it. As Heathcliff warns Ellen that his concern for his son will be 'jealous', wishing to monopolize his affection, one can almost hear the click of the prison door shutting. The father makes it clear to Ellen that his son 'is prospective owner of your place' and that the triumph of revenge will be in seeing '*my* descendent fairly lord of their estates'. Again, the use of italics serves as emphasis to the self-centred nature of this vengeance, and the picture created is one of lords and servants where Heathcliff's child will hire the children of the Grange to work on the very land which should have been their own inheritance.

The calculation involved in this revenge requires the initial outlay of finance, speculation leading to accumulation, and Heathcliff has already engaged a tutor 'to come three times a week'. The expense of this is further emphasized by adding 'from twenty miles distance'. Heathcliff is aware that superiority and power are inextricably bound up with the education, which he had not received himself, and Catherine's words of disdain must have remained rankling in his mind over the years, recalling the moment when she accused him of being 'no company at all, when people know nothing and say nothing'. (p. 69) Edgar Linton's library serves as a perpetual reminder to Heathcliff of what it was that superficially attracted Catherine, and his use of books in the coming months will play a considerable part in the exacting of his revenge. Just as Heathcliff used Hindley's drunkenness and mania for gambling, prompted by his grief at losing his wife, as tools with which to take over the Heights, he will now use the sentimentality and softness of a literary teenage romance to acquire the Grange. For this to work, Miss Catherine and Linton are going to have to indulge in a poetical interchange of books and letters which will provide the trap. After all, Catherine is not going to be caught by a boor like Hareton, and money laid out for Linton's tutor will be well spent. The extension of Heathcliff's malice is felt with the comment about ordering Hareton 'to obey him' and arranging everything 'with a view to preserve the superior and the gentleman' in Linton 'above his associates'.

In Chapter 7, a little less than 3 years later, with a combination of temptation and coercion, Catherine and Ellen enter the Heights. The temptation for Catherine is to see Heathcliff's son whom she doesn't think she has seen before, and Ellen is forced to accompany her 'struggling to release my arm'. Once inside the door, Heathcliff is quite open to Ellen about his intentions:

My design is as honest as possible. I'll in form you of its whole scope...That the two cousins may fall in love, and get married. I'm acting generously to your master; his

young chit has no expectations, and should she second
my wishes, she'll be provided for, at once, as joint successor with Linton. (p. 213)

That the theme of revenge in the novel is closely bound up
with the avarice felt by the miser, the man who counts his
money with assiduous care, and this financial sense of pay-
ing debts is evident from the early stages of Heathcliff's deg-
radation at the hands of Hindley. The image used to describe
Heathcliff's feelings at having unwittingly saved the life of
the falling baby Hareton, catching him as he is dropped by
his drunken father, is significant:

> A miser who has parted with a lucky lottery ticket for five
> shillings and finds next day he has lost in the bargain five
> thousand pounds, could not show a blanker countenance
> than he did on beholding the figure of Mr Earnshaw
> above – It expressed, plainer than words could do, the
> intensest anguish at having made himself the instrument
> of thwarting his own revenge. Had it been dark, I dare say,
> he would have tried to remedy the mistake by smashing
> Hareton's skull on the steps; but, we witnessed his salva-
> tion; and I was presently below with my precious charge
> pressed to my heart. (p. 74)

The unnatural nature of financial greed is emphasized here
by the reference to Heathcliff's 'natural impulse' to catch
the falling child. However, the detailed itemization of the
reference to the lottery ticket accompanied by the blankness
of the countenance registering the loss of greater amounts
prepares the reader for the deliberate and calculating manner of Heathcliff's revenge. In the passage, when Heathcliff
refers to tending Linton 'as carefully as your master tends
his own', we are presented with the image of the careful business man who looks after his investments.

The coveting of other people's property is central to
the theme of revenge in the novel as was illustrated when

Heathcliff considered the possibility of using Isabella's infatuation with him against Linton. Sharing his reflections with Catherine by asking if Isabella is 'her brother's heir', he prompts Catherine to add 'Abstract your mind from the subject, at present – you are too prone to covet your neighbour's goods: remember *this* neighbour's goods are mine.' Although Heathcliff appears to agree with her and to put the idea out of mind, Nellie felt certain that he 'recalled it often in the course of the evening', and she saw him 'smile to himself – grin rather – and lapse into ominous musing whenever Mrs Linton had occasion to be absent from the apartment' (p. 106). This 'ominous musing' recalls the concentration upon revenge which the young Heathcliff had indulged earlier in the novel after being beaten and imprisoned by Hindley:

> He leant his two elbows on his knees, and his chin on his hands, and remained wrapt in dumb meditation. On my enquiring the subject of his thoughts, he answered gravely –
>
> 'I'm trying to settle how I shall pay Hindley back. I don't care how long I wait, if I can only do it, at last. I hope he will not die before I do!'
>
> 'For shame, Heathcliff!' said I. 'It is for God to punish wicked people; we should learn to forgive'.
>
> 'No, God won't have the satisfaction that I shall,' he returned. 'I only wish I knew the best way! Let me alone, and I'll plan it out: while I'm thinking of that, I don't feel pain'. (p. 60)

A monomaniacal association of revenge and property haunts Heathcliff's thwarted love for Catherine, and his accusation against her is couched in terms of relative property values:

> Having levelled my palace, don't erect a hovel and complacently admire your own charity in giving me that for a home. (p. 111)

The theme of revenge extended over more than one generation may well have one of its origins in Emily Brontë's awareness of the story surrounding Elizabeth Patchett's school at Law Hill near Halifax where she had been a teacher for some 6 months between September 1838 and March 1839. The building on a high hill with panoramic views, exposed to the winds, had been erected by Jack Sharp. Early in the eighteenth century, Sharp, an orphan, had been adopted by his uncle John Walker of Walterclough Hall who owned an export business in the wool trade. Sharp gradually gained ascendance within the family by being taken on as a partner, at the expense of Walker's own sons. The excessive indulgence shown towards Sharp by his older partner encouraged the young man to become overbearing, and he gradually took over the main interests of the business. When John Walker died in 1771, his eldest son claimed the Hall back and Sharp was forced out, vowing revenge. He proceeded to build Law Hill nearby and to entice the easygoing son into a life of drunkenness and gambling. He also corrupted a cousin of the heir, degrading him in a similar manner to the one in which Heathcliff disinherits Hareton. Incidentally, Sharp's manservant was called Joseph.

Emily Brontë's reading of *Rob Roy* would have given her a lasting picture of unwavering hatred coupled with the desire for revenge as Rashleigh Osbaldistone dies venting his spleen at the end of the novel:

'I wish you only to know that the pangs of death do not alter one iota of my feelings towards you. I hate you!' he said, the expression of rage throwing a hideous glare into the eyes which were soon to be closed for ever – ' I hate you with a hatred as intense, now while I lie bleeding before you, as if my foot trod your neck.'

The bearing of grudges over a long period of time referred to in Mrs. Gaskell's story of the stone kept in the pocket for 7 years was so much a part of the psychological landscape experienced by the Brontës that the story surfaced in Charlotte's novel, *Shirley*:

> But his accomplices will take revenge on you. You do not know how the people of this country bear malice: it is the boast of some of them that they can keep a stone in their pocket seven years, turn it at the end of that time, keep it seven years longer, and hurl it, and hit their mark at last. (*Shirley* p. 123)

In *The Genesis of Wuthering Heights*, Mary Visick draws attention to how a potentially heroic theme of revenge becomes diminished in Emily Brontë's novel where the 'Lust for revenge has transformed the basilisk-eyed Gondal man into a landlord who squeezes his tenants':

> Yet avarice is what the noble crime of revenge becomes when it is transferred to the novel's actuality. There is a fine perception of moral cause-and-effect here. To strike at his enemies through their property is the only revenge possible in a world where one of these enemies is a Justice of the Peace; and the habit of avarice grows on him. (Visick p. 68)

While there is a passionate sense of violence accompanying the bloodlust of revenge, evident in Heathcliff's language when he comments to Ellen about 'painting the house-front with Hindley's blood!' (p. 48), the whole novel rises far above a Gothic story of passion and revenge. The manner in which Heathcliff completes his plans is conveyed in terms of property and ownership and 'The guest was now the master of Wuthering Heights':

> he held firm possession, and proved to the attorney, who, in his turn, proved it to Mr Linton, that Earnshaw had mortgaged every yard of land he owned for cash to supply his mania for gaming: and he, Heathcliff, was the mortgagee.

In that manner, Hareton, who should now be the first gentleman in the neighbourhood, was reduced to a state of complete dependence on his father's inveterate enemy; and lives in his own house as a servant deprived of the advantage of wages, and quite unable to right himself, because of his friendlessness, and his ignorance that he has been wronged. (p. 186)

In Mary Visick's words, Heathcliff himself 'at last, in his lust for revenge, has become a skinflint and a bully...' (Visick p. 9)

PASSAGE 6 (DEATH)

'I'll tell you what I did yesterday! I got the sexton, who was digging Linton's grave, to remove the earth off her coffin lid, and I opened it. I thought, once, I would have stayed there, when I saw her face again – it is hers yet – he had hard work to stir me; but he said it would change, if the air blew on it, so I struck one side of the coffin loose – and covered it up – not Linton's side, damn him! I wish he'd been soldered in lead – and I bribed the sexton to pull it away, when I'm laid there, and slide mine out too. I'll have it made so, and then, by the time Linton gets to us, he'll not know which is which!'

'You were very wicked, Mr Heathcliff!' I exclaimed; 'were you not ashamed to disturb the dead?'

'I disturbed nobody, Nelly,' he replied; 'and I gave some ease to myself. I shall be a great deal more comfortable now; and you'll have a better chance of keeping me underground, when I get there. Disturbed her? No! she has disturbed me, night and day, through eighteen years – incessantly – remorselessly – till yesternight – and yesternight, I was tranquil. I dreamt I was sleeping the last sleep, by that sleeper, with my heart stopped, and my cheek frozen against hers.'

'And if she had been dissolved into earth, or worse, what would you have dreamt of then?' I said.

'Of dissolving with her, and being more happy still!' he answered. 'Do you suppose I dread any change of that sort?

I expected such a transformation on raising the lid, but I'm better pleased that it should not commence till I share it. Besides, unless I had received a distinct impression of her passionless features, that strange feeling would hardly have been removed. It began oddly. You know, I was wild after she died, and eternally, from dawn to dawn, praying her to return to me – her spirit – I have a strong faith in ghosts; I have a conviction that they can, and do exist, among us!

'The day she was buried there came a fall of snow. In the evening I went to the churchyard. It blew bleak as winter – all round was solitary: I didn't fear that her fool of a husband would wander up the den so late – and no one else had business to bring them there.

'Being alone, and conscious two yards of loose earth was the sole barrier between us, I said to myself –

'"I'll have her in my arms again! If she be cold, I'll think it is this north wind that chills *me*; and if she be motionless, it is sleep."' (p. 285–6)

It is perhaps the precision of the writing in this passage from Volume II, C 15 which makes it so disturbing and lifts it beyond the world of the Gothic. As we know from the chronology laid out by Sanger, which you will find in Chapter 4 of this book, Heathcliff is referring to the incident of breaking into Catherine's coffin on the same day as the funeral of Edgar Linton, that is, some 18 years after her death and burial. As Melissa Fegan points out in her study of the character of Heathcliff, he shares some similarity with the nameless hero of Byron's poem 'The Giaour' (1813). However, whereas Byron's hero is haunted by visions of his dead lover, Emily Brontë's Heathcliff presents the reader with a picture that is considerably more unsettling:

Brontë translates Byron's fairly conventional yearning for reunion after death into something much more disturbing and sensational with the concrete details about the actual corpse of the beloved, and the suggestion of necrophilia and vampirism.

Byron's language contemplates the idea of death effecting a change upon the physical features of the dead Leila:

> Yet, Leila! yet the form is thine!
> And art thou, dearest, chang'd so much,
> As meet my eye, yet mock my touch?

The language here is reminiscent of Macbeth's 'air-drawn dagger', which appears to be substantial but which is incapable of being grasped. Byron's hero continues by wishing to 'enfold' the cold beauties of his dead lover but finds that his arms are grasping 'around a shadow prest'. Compared with this Romantic yearning for the impossible, the bringing of the past back to life, Emily Brontë's writing has a matter-of-fact exactness. First, the earth has to be removed 'off her coffin lid' before Heathcliff can look again at the face of the long-dead Catherine. The advice of the grave digger is timely: 'he said it would change, if the air blew on it,' and this is what prompts Heathcliff to strike the side of the coffin loose before covering up the corpse again. With the financial transaction (bribery) completed, we are presented with a picture of what will in effect be Catherine and Heathcliff lying dead in a double bed. There is a further gloatingly disturbing suggestion that he will be holding the corpse lovingly in his arms so tightly that the dead Edgar Linton will 'not know which is which!' This connection between love and death has, of course, an echo of the opening of Juliet's tomb in *Romeo and Juliet* where the distraught young husband uncovers the body which still seems to bear signs of life. Grasping what he thinks is Juliet's corpse, and swearing to remain in this bedchamber for ever he says:

> Arms, take your last embrace, and lips, O you
> The doors of breath, seal with a righteous kiss
> A dateless bargain to engrossing death.
>
> (Act V, scene III)

However, the physical entwining of the two corpses has another Gothic precedent closer to Emily Brontë's time in Victor Hugo's 1831 novel *Notre-Dame de Paris*. Here, the hunchbacked bell-ringer Quasimodo breaks into the charnel house to seek out the hanged corpse of his beloved gypsy, Esmerelda. When the ghoulish place is opened some time later, the decomposed body of the hunchback is found clasping the body of the girl in an embrace, which renders them both like dust when separated. That Emily Brontë knew of Hugo's work is evident from her time in Brussels, and Mrs. Gaskell records a moment in 1842 when M. Heger read Hugo's celebrated portrait of Mirabeau to the Brontë sisters before asking them to write a similar type of portrait. Emily's essay was a portrait of King Harold II of England before the battle of Hastings in 1066, and she commented upon the Englishman in terms of 'Tout en lui etait puissant'. Edward Chitham points out how this devoir provides a model for her later writing by concentrating upon 'the heroic character of the principal figure, expressed in restless movement across the metaphorical stage; the contrast between his demeanour there and in other circumstances; and the rhetorical style in which all this is expressed' (Chitham p. 62).

The idea that the ghost of the dead remains to haunt the living is emphasized in the passage by Heathcliff telling Ellen that his arrangements with the sexton will ensure that 'you'll have a better chance of keeping me underground, when I get there.' The conviction that there will be some sort of life after the physical death of the body is further highlighted by his suggestion that he will be 'sleeping the last sleep, by the sleeper, with my heart stopped, and my cheek frozen against hers'. This image endorses the feeling of the two lovers sharing the same bed, and the idea of the corpse 'dissolving' suggests a journey of metamorphosis, a movement into another world, and Heathcliff is 'better pleased that it should not commence till I share it'. The last few lines of the passage recall the night of Catherine's burial when Heathcliff was determined to hold the dead body in his arms again, and the

exactness of the 'two yards of loose earth' being the only barrier between the living and the dead becomes an anguished
reminder of the proximity between being and not being. The
ghoulish world of opening graves is then presented to us by
the directness of Heathcliff's description of what he did:

> I got a spade from the toolhouse, and began to delve
> with all my might – it scraped the coffin; I fell to work
> with my hands; the wood commenced cracking about the
> screws... (p. 286)

Emily Brontë's firm rejection of the spiritually conceived
nature of a Heaven after death is firmly placed with this
sense of the earthiness of the dead, and it finds an echo in
the dream that Catherine relates to Ellen when they are talking about the decision to marry Edgar:

> I was only going to say that heaven did not seem to be my
> home; and I broke my heart with weeping to come back
> to earth; and the angels were so angry that they flung me
> out, into the middle of the heath on the top of Wuthering
> Heights; where I woke sobbing for joy. (p. 80)

It seems that Catherine is aware that her decision to marry
Edgar and move into the financially secure world of the
Grange is akin to having died and gone to Heaven. When
she suffers her delirious outburst later, she feels that she has
been 'wrenched from the Heights' and exiled from 'what had
been my world'. Commanding Ellen to open the window,
she thinks that she can see the lights of Wuthering Heights
and wants to find her way back there:

> It's a rough journey, and a sad heart to travel it; and
> we must pass by Gimmerton Kirk, to go that journey!
> (p. 125)

It is as if she is aware that death is the only door that opens
up to allow her access to the past upon which she turned her

back. The word 'we' makes it clear that this journey through death is one which she contemplates taking *with* Heathcliff and she continues:

> We've braved its ghosts often together, and dared each other to stand among the graves and ask them to come...But Heathcliff, if I dare you now, will you venture? If you do, I'll keep you. I'll not lie there by myself; they may bury me twelve feet deep, and throw the church down over me; but I won't rest till you are with me...I never will! (ibid.)

The poem, 'Shall Earth no more inspire thee' written in May 1841 concentrates upon what Juliet Barker calls 'an important idea that was to recur in later poetry and also in *Wuthering Heights*: a longing for death that rejected conventional views of Heaven in favour of a Paradise that was as like earth as possible'. The yearning voice of loss can be heard in the second stanza

> Thy mind is ever moving
> In regions dark to thee;
> Recall its useless roving –
> Come back and dwell with me –

Pursued further in the poem of 17 July 1841, 'I see around me tombstones grey,' the world of a traditional spiritual Heaven is conjured up as a 'dazzling land above', but the resolution to remain firmly entombed in the ground is clear:

> We would not leave our native home
> For *any* world beyond the Tomb
> No – rather on thy kindly breast
> Let us be laid in lasting rest
> Or waken but to share with thee
> A mutual immortality –

73

The closing lines of the novel might seem to suggest a similar sense of reunion in death, which is connected to the physicality of the buried corpses:

> I sought, and soon discovered, the three head-stones on the slope next the moor – the middle one, grey, and half buried in heath – Edgar Linton's only harmonized by the turf, and moss creeping up its foot – Heathcliff's still bare.
>
> I lingered round them, under that benign sky; watched the moths fluttering among the heath, and hare-bells; listened to the soft wind breathing through the grass; and wondered how anyone could ever imagine unquiet slumbers, for the sleepers in that quiet earth. (p. 334)

However, we must also remind ourselves that this is the voice of Lockwood, and perhaps, he is a little unaware of the implications of his language of 'breathing', 'slumbers' and 'sleeping'. After all, one of the more dramatically vivid scenes of death is presented when Ellen discovers the corpse of Heathcliff lying by the open window in his bedroom. As if serving as a reminder of the opening of the novel when Lockwood's nightmare of the child trying to get in is made horrific by his rubbing her wrist 'to and fro till the blood ran down' (p. 25) here the window 'flapping to and fro, had grazed one hand that rested on the sill' (p. 332). Heathcliff had implored the wandering spirit of Catherine to come back, and now, his corpse possesses a 'frightful, life-like gaze of exultation'. In striking contrast with Lockwood's serene feeling that the dead lie undisturbed 'in that quiet earth', Nelly describes Heathcliff's funeral and its immediate aftermath:

> The six men departed when they had let it down into the grave: we stayed to see it covered. Hareton, with a streaming face, dug green sods, and laid them over the brown mould himself: at present it is as smooth and verdant as its companion mounds – and I hope its tenant sleeps as soundly. But the country folks, if you asked them, would

swear on their Bible that he *walks*. There are those who speak to having met him near the church, and on the moor, and even within this house – Idle tales, you'll say, and so say I. yet that old man by the kitchen fire affirms he has seen two on 'em, looking out of his chamber window, on every rainy night, since his death. (p. 333)

PASSAGE 7 (LANDSCAPE)

One of the most immediately striking aspects of *Wuthering Heights* is its remarkable lack of any lengthy descriptions of landscape despite it being clear throughout the novel that both scenery and the weather inform the characters and their actions. This section will therefore highlight shorter passages in order to bring the reader's attention to that economical and spare evocation of a sense of place that Edward Chitham refers to as 'almost Tacitean compression and compactness'.

In her Preface to the second edition of the novel, Charlotte Brontë referred to the 'rusticity' of *Wuthering Heights* and commented that 'It is Moorish, and wild, and knotty as the root of heath.' In order to make clear that this sense of the importance of landscape and setting is in no way provided as simply an example of the picturesque she continues:

Ellis Bell did not describe as one whose eye and taste alone found pleasure in the prospect; her native hills were far more to her than a spectacle; they were what she lived in, and by, as much as the wild birds, their tenants, or as the heather, their produce.

The vivid re-creation of weather and landscape, intimately known by one who walked the moors, is evident from the short evocation of a harsh West Yorkshire November that appears in the second chapter of the novel:

On that bleak hill top the earth was hard with a black frost, and the air made me shiver through every limb.

> Being unable to remove the chain, I jumped over, and, running up the flagged causeway bordered with straggling gooseberry bushes, knocked vainly for admittance, till my knuckles tingled, and the dogs howled. (p. 9)

The reader is struck here by the simplicity of the alliteration, 'bleak' and 'black', followed by the pervasive cold, which gets in everywhere. The inability to remove the chain (iron) is followed by the harshness of the stone flags, the 'straggling' bushes which do not seem to offer much sense of life and Lockwood's fingers tingling with cold as he vainly tries to seek shelter from the cold. The almost poetical sharpness of this writing conveys the effects of the weather upon character and the feeling that the landscape's inhospitable refusal to accommodate itself to human needs is further emphasized when Lockwood feels himself increasingly trapped in the Heights:

> A sorrowful sight I saw; dark night coming down prematurely, and sky and hills mingled in one bitter whirl of wind and suffocating snow. (p. 14)

The weather here seems to act as a threatening form of imprisonment with its suggestion of 'suffocating', and this sense of danger is highlighted by the cadence of the phrase 'coming down prematurely' with its implication of an unstoppable force. Movement of weather like this is used again for an urgent emotional effect later in the novel when Catherine is suffering from delirium in her bedroom at the Grange after the major confrontation between Edgar and Heathcliff:

> 'That's a turkey's,' she murmured to herself; 'and this is a wild-duck's; and this is a pigeon's. Ah, they put pigeons' feathers in the pillows – no wonder I couldn't die. Let me take care to throw it on the floor when I lie down. And here is a moorcock's; and this – I should know it among a thousand – it's a lapwing's. Bonny bird; wheeling over

our heads in the middle of the moor. It wanted to get to its nest, for the clouds touched the swells, and it felt rain coming. This feather was picked up from the heath, the bird was not shot – we saw its nest in the winter, full of little skeletons. Heathcliff set a trap over it, and the old ones dare not come. (p. 121)

As is noted in the Clarendon edition of the novel, edited by Hilda Marsden and Ian Jack, pigeon feathers have a particular connection with folklore as is revealed in Richard Blakeborough's *Wit, Character, Folklore and Customs of the North Riding of Yorkshire*:

> The soul cannot free itself if the dying person has been laid on a bed containing pigeon feathers... Instances are on record of pigeon feathers having been placed in a small bag, and thrust under dying persons to hold them back until the arrival of some loved one.

The ominous sense in the fast-approaching change of weather is felt in the word 'wheeling', going round and round without getting to where it needs to be, and the imminence of the rain is caught with the clouds touching the bare upland hills.

The most detailed scene where a sense of landscape and weather are interwoven with character occurs in Volume II, Chapter 8 where Catherine and Ellen fill up their time one afternoon in autumn by walking in the park. Catherine's epistolary romance with Linton has been stopped, and she is clearly both listless and bored as well as concerned about the increasing ill health of her father who had caught a cold from being out in the 'chill and damp' of an evening's ramble:

> On an afternoon in October, or the beginning of November, a fresh watery afternoon, when the turf and paths were rustling with moist, withered leaves, and the cold, blue sky was half hidden by clouds, dark grey streamers, rapidly

mounting from the west, and boding abundant rain; I requested my young lady to forgo her ramble because I was certain of showers. She refused; and I unwillingly donned a cloak, and took my umbrella to accompany her on a stroll to the bottom of the park; a formal walk which she generally affected if low-spirited; and that she invariably was when Mr Edgar had been worse than ordinary; a thing never known from his confession, but guessed both by her and me from his increased silence, and the melancholy of his countenance. (p. 226)

The vivid feeling of an autumn afternoon is conveyed by the sound of the damp leaves while the fast-moving threat of bad weather seems unstoppable as it mounts 'rapidly' from the west with 'dark grey streamers': the light of day is disappearing. The melancholy of the scene is further emphasized by the 'withered' leaves. In an attempt to distract Catherine from sad thoughts, Ellen looks at the high bank that runs alongside the road; but before she makes her comments about a flower that she notices there, she presents a digressive picture of life some time ago:

On one side of the road rose a high, rough bank, where hazels and stunted oaks, with their roots half-exposed, held uncertain tenure: the soil was too loose for the latter; and strong winds had blown some nearly horizontal. In summer, Miss Catherine delighted to climb along these trunks, and sit in the branches, swinging twenty feet above the ground; and I, pleased with her agility, and her light, childish heart, still considered it proper to scold every time I caught her at such an elevation; but so that she knew there was no necessity for descending. From dinner to tea she would lie in her breeze-rocked cradle, doing nothing except singing old songs – my nursery lore – to herself, or watching the birds, joint tenants, feed and entice their young ones to fly, or nestling with closed lids, half thinking, half dreaming, happier than words can express. (p. 227)

The picture of innocence presented here is made all the more moving because of its fragility and vulnerability. The branches of the trees, which become a child's cradle, are insecure with their 'roots half-exposed'. It will be Catherine's own family roots that will bring about her initial destruction as they are 'exposed' to the scrutiny of the inevitable Heathcliff, whose own name provides two evocations of the wilder side of the natural world. The fact that the oaks are stunted inevitably brings to mind the thwarted and twisted upbringing of Hareton and echoes the comment made to Ellen by Heathcliff when he decides to bring up Hindley's child as his own:

> 'Now, my bonny lad, you are *mine*! And we'll see if one tree won't grow as crooked as another, with the same wind to twist it!' (p. 185)

The child's sense of safety while her cradle rocks is associated with 'watching the birds', and as the image is also of them feeding their young, it inevitably calls to mind the previously quoted image of the lapwings where the parents cannot feed their young out of fear of the trap set by Heathcliff.

As Ellen moves her attention back to the present, she points out a flower on the bank for Catherine to see:

> 'Look, Miss!' I exclaimed, pointing to a nook under the roots of one twisted tree. 'Winter is not here yet. There's a little flower, up yonder, the last bud from the multitude of blue-bells that clouded those turf steps in July with a lilac mist. Will you clamber up, and pluck it to show to papa?'
>
> Cathey stared a long time at the lonely blossom trembling in its earthy shelter, and replied, at length –
>
> 'No, I'll not touch it – but it looks melancholy, does it not, Ellen?'
>
> 'Yes,' I observed, 'about as starved and sackless as you – your cheeks are bloodless; let us take hold of hands

and run. You're so low, I dare say I shall keep up with you'.

'No,' she repeated, and continued sauntering on, pausing, at intervals, to muse over a bit of moss, or a tuft of blanched grass, or a fungus spreading its bright orange among the heaps of brown foliage; and, ever and anon, her hand was lifted to her averted face. (p. 227)

Catherine's comment about the lone flower looking 'starved and sackless' ('frozen and dispirited' according to Pauline Nestor's note) has an eerie sense of premonition as if she can foresee her own lonely position in the Heights of the future when she is exiled from her own home.

The poems that Emily wrote when she was herself feeling exiled as a teacher in the school at Law Hill provide a similar nostalgic yearning for the cradle-like safety of the moorland scenes around Haworth. 'A little while, a little while', dated 4 December 1838, calls for the mind to be allowed to return to a previous time and place:

> There is a spot 'mid barren hills
> Where winter howls and driving rain
> But if the dreary tempest chills
> There is a light that warms again
>
> The house is old, the trees are bare
> And moonless bends the misty dome
> But what on earth is half so dear –
> So longed for as the hearth of home?
>
> The mute bird sitting on the stone,
> The dank moss dripping from the wall,
> The garden-walk with weeds o'ergrown
> I love them – how I love them all!

The slightly earlier composition, 11 November, also has a resonance with Catherine's state of mind in her lassitude that precedes her enforced exile at the Heights, an exile that is only ended with the approaching union with the deracinated Hareton:

> What language can utter the feeling
> That rose when, in exile afar,
> On the brow of a lonely hill kneeling
> saw the brown heath growing there.
>
> It was scattered and stunted, and told me
> That soon even that would be gone
> It whispered, 'The grim walls enfold me
> I have bloomed in my last summer's sun'.

This yearning to be part of the landscape that surrounded Emily is what prompts Charlotte to comment in her Preface:

> My sister Emily loved the moors. Flowers brighter than the rose bloomed in the blackest of the heath for her; out of a sullen hollow in a livid hill-side her mind could make an Eden. She found in the bleak solitude many and dear delights; and not the least and best loved was – liberty.

However, no mention of Eden can avoid the corollary of the Fall, and the pervading atmosphere of *Wuthering Heights* is one of loss.

PASSAGE 8 (LOVE)

There are four passages chosen here to illustrate different aspects of the theme of love in *Wuthering Heights,* and through their remarkable contrasts they reveal a clear progression within the novel which may help to account for that distinctive sense of release the reader feels by the time the end of the generational story has been reached.

1

'You must not go!' she exclaimed energetically.

'I must and shall!' he replied in a subdued voice.

'No,' she persisted, grasping the handle; 'not yet, Edgar Linton sit down, you shall not leave me in that temper. I should be miserable, all night, and I won't be miserable for you!'

'Can I stay after you have struck me?' asked Linton.

Catherine was mute.

'You've made me afraid, and ashamed of you,' he continued; 'I'll not come here again!'

Her eyes began to glisten and her lids to twinkle.

'And you told a deliberate untruth!' he said.

'I didn't!' she cried, recovering her speech. 'I did nothing deliberately – Well, go, if you please – get away! And now I'll cry – I'll cry myself sick!'

She dropped down on her knees by a chair and set to weeping in serious earnest.

Edgar persevered in his resolution as far as the court; there, he lingered. I resolved to encourage him.

'Miss is dreadfully wayward, sir!' I called out. 'As bad as any marred child – you'd better be riding home, or else she will be sick only to grieve us.'

The soft thing looked askance through the window – he possessed the power to depart, as much as a cat possesses the power to leave a mouse half killed, or a bird half eaten –

Ah, I thought, there will be no saving him – He's doomed, and flies to his fate! (p. 71)

This passage from Volume I, Chapter 8 records a moment during the courtship of Catherine and Edgar, and it presents us with an illustration of a clear conflict of wills, a picture of what in other circumstances could be regarded as an adolescent lovers' tiff. However, what haunts the text is an incipient quality of violence and a determination to use self-destruction as a tool in order to get one's own way. Catherine has just been caught out pinching Ellen 'with a prolonged wrench' following it up by slapping her with 'a stinging blow that filled both eyes with water'. Catherine's outburst of temper is then directed towards the gentlemanly and rather priggish Edgar as she slaps him too 'in a way that could not be mistaken for jest'. Edgar's haughty and controlled response emphasizes his Thrushcross Grange manners as he insists (both 'must' and 'shall') 'in a subdued voice' that he can no longer stay at the Heights as a visitor. One can hear the latent magistrate's voice in his cool appraisal of the scene as he tells Catherine that he is 'ashamed' of her and affirms his intention of ceasing their courtship with a decisive 'I'll not come here again!' At this stage of the action, Catherine's resort is to feminine vulnerability as her 'eyes began to glisten and her lids to twinkle', and the flirtatious undertone to that word 'twinkle' prepares us for the inevitable outcome. Exculpating herself from any responsibility for what has happened ('I did nothing deliberately'), she takes the upper hand as the victim who is now being mistreated. If Edgar leaves her, then **he** must take responsibility for the awful consequences as she cries herself sick. To clinch her victory, she 'dropped down on her knees by a chair and set to weeping in real earnest'. Given the masterful manner in which Catherine has played the scene, it comes as no surprise that Edgar lingers in the courtyard before making the irrevocable error of looking through the window and being drawn back to the scene that Catherine has twisted round into being his fault. Her vulnerability, as if she is a 'mouse half killed, or a bird half eaten', is her strength, and in one of the novel's most disturbing images she clearly appeals to Edgar's violent sense of his own power. Ellen refers to him as a 'soft thing' not only because of his lack of determination to leave Catherine but also in emphasis of his being like a cat, playfully destructive.

While staying at the Pensionnat Heger in 1842, Emily had written a devoir on the subject of cats for M. Heger suggesting that their similarities with human beings were connected with their hypocrisy, cruelty and ingratitude. Juliet Barker suggests that a 'cat's hypocrisy is what humans call

politeness' and quotes from the Brussels essay in a transla-
tion kept by the Brontë Society Transactions:

> ... and anyone who does not employ it to disguise his true
> feelings would soon be driven out of society.

In Chapter 12 when Catherine is again avoiding her responsibility, this time for having assisted in the physical confrontation between her husband and Heathcliff, she locks herself
in her room and after 2 days announces that 'she believed
she was dying'. The power that she believes lurks in self-
harming is made clear by Ellen's comment that she 'set down'
these words 'as a speech meant for Edgar's ears'. Whether or
not we trust this comment from Ellen as narrator, what is
clear is that Edgar makes no rush to find out how his preg-
nant wife is doing after her outburst and his association with
the civilized world of politeness is emphasized by Ellen's reference to his being occupied in the library 'among his books'.
One can almost feel the petulance of 'the soft thing' as it
allows its half-killed prey to suffer.

2

**'What were the use of my creation if I were entirely con-
tained here? My great miseries in this world have been
Heathcliff's miseries, and I watched and felt each from the
beginning; my great thought in living is himself. If all else
perished, and *he* remained, I should still continue to be; and,
if all else remained, and he were annihilated, the Universe
would turn to a mighty stranger. I should not seem part of
it. My love for Linton is like the foliage in the woods. Time
will change it, I'm well aware, as winter changes the trees –
my love for Heathcliff resembles the eternal rocks beneath
– a source of little visible delight, but necessary. Nelly, I
am Heathcliff – he's always, always in my mind – not as a
pleasure, any more than I am a pleasure to myself – but, as
my own being – so, don't talk of our separation again – it is
impracticable...' (p. 81–2)**

This is an extract from the long conversation Catherine has with Ellen in Volume I, Chapter 9, and it concludes the discussion concerning the relative merits of marrying Edgar as opposed to maintaining a close relationship with Heathcliff. In her contribution to *Form and Function in the Novel*, Dorothy Van Ghent suggests that the passionate love exemplified by Catherine and Heathcliff is an 'astonishingly ravenous and possessive, perfectly amoral love', which 'belongs to that realm of the imagination where myths are created' (Van Ghent p. 155 – 6). This reference to the elemental quality of love is echoed in Katherine Frank's biography, subtitled appropriately 'A Chainless Soul' where she refers to Emily Bronte's concept of love in the following terms:

> No social or religious forms bound her. Love, for her, was essentially an amoral power, like an immutable force of nature. It had its own time and seasons and was no respecter of artificial human creations such as matrimony. (Frank p. 131)

Catherine's imaginative realization that her identification with Heathcliff transcends the temporal is registered by the use of the word 'world', which suggests much more than the simple environment of the moors surrounding the Heights. This sense of standing apart from the natural environment is continued by her suggestion that if everything in that environment were to die and yet Heathcliff were to continue to live, then 'I should still continue to be.' Here, the mythical quality of the attachment between the two is emphasized by their figures being raised above the constraints of human mortality and the natural effects of time. Again by using the term 'Universe', Catherine brings to the fore a concept of Time and Space, which stretches far beyond the local, and it paves the way for the contrast between seasonal transitions and elemental fixity. The suggestion of her love for Edgar being comparable to 'the foliage in the woods' hints at a world of romantic trysts amid pastoral scenes, whereas the conjunction of Heathcliff with 'eternal rocks beneath' not only conveys a harsh implication of permanence but also a feeling that the connection between the two people has a subterranean presence, which underlies everything else. This imaginative realization of permanence may well reflect the author's reading of the role of the secondary imagination in Coleridge's 1817 autobiography *Biographia Literaria* where he asserts that it 'dissolves, diffuses, dissipates, in order to recreate... It is essentially *vital*, even as all objects (*as* objects) are essentially fixed and dead'.

The conversation between Catherine and Nelly about comparative loves suggests that the type of love experienced between Catherine and Heathcliff transcends the social and human limitations of time passing, a love that is far beyond the world of romance, and it recalls Emily Brontë's poem 'No coward soul is mine,' which concludes:

> Though Earth and Moon were gone
> And suns and universes ceased to be
> And thou wert left alone
> Every Existence would exist in thee
>
> There is not room for Death
> Nor atom that his might could render void
> Since thou art Being and Breath
> And what thou art may never be destroyed

Although it was not published until 1850, the poem is dated 2 January 1846, and in *The Birth of Wuthering Heights*, Edward Chitham argues that the writing of the passage from the novel may well have been also in the spring of that year. In *The Genesis of Wuthering Heights*, Mary Visick also refers to the poem in order to suggest that 'Catherine betrays what amounts to a mystical vocation, for social position and romantic love' and that this decision is central to the tragedy contained within the novel.

READING *WUTHERING HEIGHTS*

3

> She also got a trick of coming down early in the morning, and lingering about the kitchen, as if she were expecting the arrival of something; and she had a small drawer in a cabinet in the library which she would trifle over for hours, and whose key she took special care to remove when she left it.
>
> One day, as she inspected this drawer, I observed that the playthings, and trinkets, which recently formed its contents, were transmuted into bits of folded paper.
>
> My curiosity and suspicions were roused; I determined to take a peep at her mysterious treasures; so, at night, as soon as she and my master were safe upstairs, I searched and readily found among my house keys, one that would fit the lock. Having opened, in emptied the whole contents into my apron, and took them with me to examine at leisure in my own chamber.
>
> Though I could not but suspect, I was still surprised to discover that they were a mass of correspondence, daily almost, it must have been, from Linton Heathcliff, answers to documents forwarded by her. The earlier dated were embarrassed and short; gradually, however, they expanded into copious love letters, foolish as the age of the writer rendered natural, yet with touches, here and there, which I thought were borrowed from a more experienced source.
>
> Some of them struck me as singularly odd compounds of ardour, and flatness; commencing in strong feeling, and concluding in the affected, wordy way that a school-boy might use to a fancied, incorporeal sweetheart.
>
> Whether they satisfied Cathy, I don't know, but they appeared very worthless trash to me. (p. 222-3)

This episode in Volume II, Chapter 7, presents the reader with a picture of a childish romance between two 16-year olds conducted by letter. Any sense of childish naivety is undercut by the ominous undertones which appear when Ellen relates that there were touches in the letters 'which I thought were borrowed from a more experienced source'. While this may of course refer to the adoption of styles inherited from a diet of reading epistolary novels of romance, there is a suggestion that the figure whose presence lies behind the correspondence is Heathcliff's. The mixture of innocence and childishness in the world of young Catherine's correspondence with Linton is emphasized from the beginning of the passage by the use of the word 'trick' and the picture of the young girl trifling 'for hours' over the little locked drawer. Ellen notes that that 'playthings' and 'trinkets' have been replaced by the voluminous correspondence, which is little more than a bridge between the world of childhood and the world of adolescent romance. Ellen's contempt for the type of writing exposed in these letters could not be made clearer when she refers to the 'affected, wordy way that a school-boy might use to a fancied incorporeal sweetheart' and concludes by condemning them as 'very worthless trash'. The idea that phrases and sentiments used in the letters are reflections of the diet of reading consumed by the young lovers is further emphasized by Ellen's comment on page 224 when she confronts Catherine to tell her that 'A fine bundle of trash you study in your leisure hours, to be sure – Why, it's good enough to be printed!' However, one of the most powerful aspects of this 'trash' lies in the way in which it allows Heathcliff to pervert naivety in order to gain his own ends. As we know from his courtship of Isabella, he is quite capable of subterfuge in order to achieve what he wants as Ellen had already noticed:

> Heathcliff had not the habit of bestowing a single unnecessary civility on Miss Linton, I knew. Now, as soon as he beheld her, his first precaution was to take a sweeping survey of the house-front. I was standing by the kitchen window, but I drew out of sight. He then stept across the pavement to her, and said something: she seemed embarrassed, and desirous of getting away; to prevent it, he laid

his hand on her arm: she averted her face; he apparently put some question which she had no mind to answer. There was another rapid glance at the house, and supposing himself unseen, the scoundrel had the impudence to embrace her. (p. 110)

Here, the prospective lover uses the precaution of not being seen from the house before adopting the attitude of forceful intimacy, laying his hand on her arm and then, after another 'rapid glance' around, embracing her. Throughout the scene, Isabella appears passive, and a sharp contrast between romantic passion and the grim reality beneath is provided when we recall the earlier image of warning used by Catherine as she tries to make her sister-in-law understand that there is a significant difference between the two:

I'd as soon put that little canary into the park on a winter's day as recommend you to bestow your heart on him. (p. 101)

The subterfuge of romantic letter writing is placed in its rightful context when Catherine visits Linton some time after the correspondence has ceased and is greeted by the boy's comment:

'Why didn't you come before?' he said. 'You should have come, instead of writing. It tired me dreadfully, writing those long letters.'

This comment stands in stark contrast with the words used by Heathcliff to Catherine when she is outside the gates of Thrushcross Grange on page 230:

Two or three months since, were you not in the habit of writing to Linton? making love in play, eh? You deserved, both of you, flogging for that! You especially, the elder, and less sensitive, as it turns out. 'ive got your letters, and if you give me any pertness, I'll send them to your father. I presume you grew weary of the amusement, and dropped it, didn't you? Well, you dropped Linton with it, into a Slough of Despond. He was in earnest – in love – really. As true as I live, he's dying for you – breaking his heart at your fickleness, not figuratively, but actually.

As with his words of courtship to Isabella, Heathcliff is unaware that he is being overheard here and growls about not being aware that 'there were eaves-droppers'.

4

I could both see them and hear them talk before I entered; and, looked and listened in consequence, being moved thereto by a mingled sense of curiosity, and envy that grew as I lingered.

'Con-*trary*!' said a voice, as sweet as a silver bell – 'That for the third time, you dunce! I'm not going to tell you again – Recollect, or I pull your hair!'

'Contrary, then,' answered another, in deep, but softened tones. 'And now, kiss me, for minding so well.'

'No, read it over first correctly, without a single mistake.'

The male speaker began to read – he was a young man, respectably dressed, and seated at a table, having a book before him. His handsome features glowed with pleasure, and his eyes kept impatiently wandering from the page to a small white hand over his shoulder, which recalled him by a smart slap on the cheek, whenever its owner detected such signs of inattention.

Its owner stood behind; her light shining ringlets blending, at intervals, with his brown locks, as she bent to superintend his studies; and her face – it was lucky he could not see her face, or he would never have been so steady – I could, and I bit my lip, in spite, at having thrown away the chance I might have had, of doing something besides staring at its smiting beauty.

The task was done, not free from further blunders, but the pupil claimed a reward and received at least five kisses, which, however, he generously returned. Then, they came to the door, and from their conversation, I judged they were about to issue out and have a walk on the moors. (p. 304)

Lockwood's record of what he sees through the window of the Heights as he returns to the area in September 1802 (Volume II, Chapter 18) asserts a love between two young people, which has an air of flirtation and romance than is free from corruption. The scene is immediately preceded by Lockwood noticing some significant changes at Wuthering Heights. First, he didn't have to climb the gate or knock since 'it yielded to my hand', and his immediate response to this direct contrast with his first two visits to the place is to say 'That is an improvement!' This moment is almost immediately followed by his awareness of 'a fragrance of stocks and wall flowers, wafted on the air, from amongst the homely fruit trees.' The fact that flowers and fruit subsist side by side allows us to recognize that love has not superseded the function of a farm and that therefore what we are going to witness is what Dorothy Van Ghent has called a 'culturally viable kind of love between Cathy and Hareton'. Again, there is a reference to the 'doors and lattices' being open, and Lockwood stares with a feeling of envy onto a scene that emphasizes his own isolation from love. In the opening pages of the novel, he had recorded his 'reputation of deliberate heartlessness' when he stepped back from a romance despite having encouraged it, and now, he is condemned to witness a scene that makes him bite his lip 'at having thrown away the chance I might have had'.

The flirtatious behaviour as Catherine is teaching Hareton to read takes its teasing warmth from its direct contrast with what has gone before. For instance, the young teacher threatens to pull her young charge's hair if he doesn't get the pronunciation of a word correct, and she recalls his attention to the lesson by 'a smart slap on the cheek'. This serves as a reminder of the time when Catherine was kidnapped by Heathcliff in Volume II, Chapter 13, and he administered 'a shower of terrific slaps on both sides of the head' (p. 268), which leave her putting her 'two hands to her temples' looking 'just as if she were not sure whether her ears were off or on'. The scene that Lockwood witnesses has a playfulness which encourages Hareton's 'handsome features' to glow 'with pleasure', and the intertwining of the lovers is echoed by Catherine's 'shining ringlets blending, at intervals, with his brown locks, as she bent to superintend his studies'.

There are echoes perhaps in this passage of the opening stanzas of the first poem that Brontë wrote in Brussels, dated 17 May 1842, which deals with love repeated over two generations:

> In the same place, when Nature wore
> The same celestial glow;
> I'm sure I've seen those forms before
> But many springs ago;
>
> And only *he* had locks of light
> And *she* had raven hair,
> While now, his curls are dark as night
> And hers, as morning fair.

Here, there is the theme of love repeated over two generations, the first time tragically, with differences expressed by the colouring of hair. In her notes to the Penguin edition of *The Complete Poems*, Janet Gezari suggests that 'the subject of this poem . . . is the survivor's response to death':

> Like *Wuthering Heights*, this poem considers the possibility that the pain of those who have been left behind can recall the dead to life. The image of the two children, one dark, one light, looks ahead to the dark and fair pairs in *Wuthering Heights*, Hareton and Catherine Linton and (with the colouring reversed) Edgar Linton and Cathy Earnshaw. (*Poems* p. 268)

PASSAGE 9 (RELIGION)

"'Nelly," he said, "we's hae a Crahner's 'quest enah, at ahr
folks. One on 'em's a'most getten his finger cut off wi'hauding
t'other froo' sticking hisseln loike a cawlf. That's maister,
yah knaw, ut's soa up uh going tuh t'grand 'sizes. He's noan
feard uh t' Bench uh judges, norther Paul, nut Peter, nur
John, not Mathew, not noan on 'em, nut he!... This is t' way
on't – up at sun-dahn; dice, brandy, cloised shutters, and
can'le lught till next day, at nooin – then, t' fooil gangs ban-
ning un' raving tuh his cham'er, making dacent fowks dig
thur fingers i' thur lugs fur varray shaume; un' the knave,
wah, he carn cahnt his brass, un' ate, un' sleep, un' off tuh
his neighbour's tuh gossip wi' t' wife. I' course, he tells Dame
Catherine hah hor fathur's goold runs intuh his pocket, and
hur fathur's son gallops dahn t' Broad road, while he flees
afore tuh open t' pikes? (p. 103)

This passage from Volume I, Chapter 10, gives the reader
one of the most vivid and dramatic examples of the Calvinist
world of Joseph, with its echoes of seventeenth-century Low
Church Nonconformist pamphleteering and the writing of
John Bunyan, which was well known in the Brontë household. The world of allegory and mystery that is brought to
life in Joseph's account of what goes on in Wuthering Heights
as Heathcliff helps to corrupt the drunken and aimless
Hindley brings to mind an incident recorded by Charlotte
on 22 June 1830, which is reprinted in Juliet Barker's *The
Brontes*. At half-past nine in the morning, there was a knock
on the door of the Parsonage and an old man asked to see
the parson. On being told that he was in bed unwell, the old
man simply said:

The LORD desires me to say that the bridegroom is coming & that he must prepare to meet him; that the cords are
about to be loosed & the golden Bowl broken, the Pitcher.
broken at the fountain & the wheel stopped at the cistern.
(Barker p. 168)

Having made this announcement the man went away and Charlotte concluded 'that he was some fanatical enthusiast, well-meaning perhaps but utterly ignorant of true piety'. Joseph's language is certainly that of the religious enthusiast as he contemplates those around him going to Hell. He sees religious judgement in terms of physical reality, and Hindley will soon be going up before the Grand Assizes where his crimes will receive what they have earned. When Joseph mentions the Coroner's Inquest, the Assizes and the Bench, he brings the physical reality of life after death firmly to the fore just as the image of Heathcliff preventing Hindley from destroying himself in a fit of manic depression is seen in terms of a physical fight where one man has 'a'most getten his finger cut off wi' hauding t'other froo sticking hisseln loike a cawlf'. The figures of both Heathcliff and Hindley being young dissolutes is emphasized not only by the image of the calf but also by the former being referred to as 'yon bonny lad Heathcliff'. This image of the younger man leading the elder stepbrother into perdition, where for Joseph it is not just the house and lands that are at stake but the eternal soul as well, is given a dramatic presence that could exist within a Medieval Morality Play. Hindley seeks to 'set his brazened face' against the judges (St. Paul, St. Peter, St. John, St. Matthew) while Heathcliff 'can girn a laugh, as weel's onybody at a raight divil's jest'. Similarly, the picture of Hindley galloping 'dahn t'Broad road' with Heathcliff flying in front of him 'tuh open t'pikes' could appear in one of the Medieval scenes of chase such as at the end of Chaucer's 'The Nun's Priest's Tale' where the people 'yolleden as feendes doon in helle.' This dramatically vivid language of religion is central to the 1611 King James Bible and the image of Hindley riding manically on horseback down the broad road towards his doom refers to Chapter 7 of 'The Gospel According to St. Matthew':

Enter ye in at the strait gate, for wide is the gate, and broad is the way that leadeth to destruction, and many there be which goe in thereat.

Given this almost gleeful picture of approaching damnation which Joseph offers to Ellen as an account of what is going on at the Heights, it comes as no surprise when we learn of his reaction to Heathcliff's death:

> 'Th' divil's harried off his soul,' he cried, 'and he muh hev his carcass intuh t'bargin, for ow't Aw care! Ech! what a wicked un he looks girnning at death!' and the old sinner grinned in mockery. (p. 332)

The satisfaction that Joseph feels throughout the novel at his own self-righteousness and the failings of others is emphasized here by his mocking of the grin that is on the dead man's face. This behaviour is in keeping with the account of life at the Heights given by Ellen early on:

> He was, and is yet, most likely, the wearisomest, self-righteous Pharisee that ever ransacked a Bible to rake the promises to himself, and fling the curses on his neighbours. (p. 42)

The agricultural image used here is entirely in accord with the way in which religion is perceived as a physical aspect of the environment, and Joseph is seen as one of the Lord's Chosen who has 'a vocation to be where he had plenty of wickedness to reprove' (p. 65). This physical reality that ensures that religion is seen as an integral part of the farming community finds one of its most striking images in Joseph's use of the Bible as a serviceable object upon which to sort out the day's financial business:

> ... he solemnly spread his large Bible on the table, and overlaid it with dirty bank-notes from his pocket book, the produce of the day's transactions. (p. 312)

In one sense, this may appear to be a misuse of the Bible and Melissa Fegan goes so far as to say that 'he has desecrated

the holy book by making it a repository for dirty money.'
However, the Bible has a living presence within the farmer's
house, and in 'A fresh Approach to *Wuthering Heights*', Q.
D. Leavis suggests that Joseph's 'duty to the farm, to his
master, and to God's laws, are not separate duties in his
mind but form together as a rule of life'.

Joseph's distrust of women seems to go hand-in-hand
with his religious attitudes and the picture he gives in
the passage of Heathcliff counting his ill-gotten gains
after the night's gambling before catching some food and
sleep, and then 'off tuh his neighbour's tuh gossip wi' t'
wife' adds a distinctly mundane perspective to the world
of passion. Joseph's opinion of women as lost souls who
will be damned is firmly placed for us near the opening
of the novel when Lockwood found himself trapped in
the Heights on the occasion of his second visit. Entering
the room, the old servant sees Catherine burning some
matches and says:

'Aw wonder hagh yah can faishon tuh stand thear
i'idleness un war, when all on 'em's goan aght! Bud yah're
a nowt, and it's noa use talking – yah'll niver mend uh yer
ill ways; bud goa raight tuh t'divil, like yer mother afore
ye!' (p. 15)

Joseph's harsh way of living and his contempt for idleness
are bound up with a primitive sense of religious superstition,
and it is not difficult for Catherine to answer him back by
threatening him with spells, convincing him that she has the
powers of a witch:

'You scandalous old hypocrite!' she replied. 'Are you not
afraid of being carried away bodily, whenever you mention
the devil's name? I warn you to refrain from provoking me,
or I'll ask your abduction as a special favour. Stop, look
here, Joseph,' she continued, taking a long, dark book from
a shelf. 'I'll show you how far I've progressed in the Black

Art – I shall soon be competent to make a clear house of it. the red cow didn't die by chance; and your rheumatism can hardly be reckoned among providential visitations!' (p. 15)

Joseph's immediate and only response to this threat is to gasp 'may the Lord deliver us from evil!'

The physical manifestation of God's power is central to Joseph's beliefs, and the clearest example of this occurs on the night when Heathcliff runs away in Book I, Chapter 9. With a direct echo of the night of Duncan's murder in *Macbeth* where 'our chimneys were blown down' (Act II, scene III), the stormy night hits the Heights and 'a huge bough fell across the roof' knocking down 'a portion of the east chimney-stack, sending a clatter of stones and soot into the kitchen fie'. Joseph's reaction to what he sees as the work of God is to fall to his knees:

We thought a bolt had fallen in the middle of us, and Joseph swung onto his knees, beseeching the Lord to remember the Patriarchs Noah and Lot; and, as in former times, spare the righteous, though he smote the ungodly. (p. 84)

For him, the world of religious belief and his immediate physical surroundings are completely interwoven in a way that John Bunyan creates in *Pilgrim's Progress* and other works. For example, in *The Life and Death of Mr. Badman,* Bunyan records the world of the dissolute where drunkenness is accompanied with

Oaths, blasphemies, lies, revellings, whorings, brawlings; it is a wonder to me that any that live in that sin should escape such a blow from Heaven, that should tumble them into their graves. Besides, when I consider also how, when they are as drunk as beasts, they, without all fear of danger, will ride like bedlams and madmen, even as if they did dare God to meddle with them if he durst, for their being drunk.

The physical reality of religion in the novel is also given a central place through the description of the chapel, which appears in Lockwood's first dream:

> We came to the chapel – I have passed it really in my walks, twice or thrice: it lies in a hollow, between two hills – an elevated hollow – near a swamp, whose peaty moisture is said to answer all the purposes of embalming on the few corpses deposited there. The roof has been kept whole hitherto, but, as the clergyman's stipend is only twenty pounds per annum, and a house with two rooms, threatening speedily to determine into one, no clergyman will undertake the duties of pastor, especially as it is reported that his flock would rather let him starve than increase the living by one penny from their own pockets. (p. 23)

This 'kirk' also dominates the end of the novel as Lockwood passes 'beneath its walls' and saw that 'decay had made progress, even in seven months – many a window showed black gaps deprived of glass; and slates jutted off, here and there, beyond the right line of the roof, to be gradually worked off in coming autumn storms.' (p. 334)

Since much of the physical presence of religion in the novel is bound up with Joseph's harsh dialect, it is possibly Charlotte's concern that the London audience should not feel excluded that prompted her letter of 29 September 1850 to the publisher W. S. Williams announcing her intention of republishing *Wuthering Heights* while making it clear that she felt that Joseph's dialect speech needed to be put into more acceptable English:

> I should wish to revise the proofs, if it be not too great an inconvenience to send them. It seems to me advisable to modify the orthography of the old servant Joseph's

speeches; for though as it stands it exactly renders the Yorkshire dialect to a Yorkshire ear, yet I am sure Southerns must find it unintelligible; and thus one of the most graphic characters in the book is lost on them.

That said, Joseph's rough eloquence is central to the bringing to life, a world where superstition and a rigid belief in the Old Testament inform the day-to-day life of the hill-farmers and with this in mind it is worth recalling the first appendix which Q. D. Leavis added to her 'Fresh Approach' essay. Investigating the traditional culture of the Yorkshire moorlands, she selected as an example J. H. Dixon's *Chronicles and Stories of the Craven Dales*, which were serialized between 1853 and 1857. In the introduction to the 1881 reprint of these stories, the Reverend Robert Collyer refers to a funeral where a farmer is 'laid away as he had lived, with all the old rites and observances about his dust':

Then as they bore him to his burial along the green shadowy lanes to Bolton they sang old funeral chants Job might have written, and Jeremiah set to music, they were so shorn of all that sheds a new radiance on death and the grave.

STUDY QUESTION

1. Choose one passage from each of the two volumes of the Penguin edition of *Wuthering Heights* and write a close critical analysis of them, trying to bring out how each of the two passages relates to the themes and styles of the novel as a whole.

CHAPTER 4

CRITICAL RECEPTION AND
PUBLISHING HISTORY

William Smith Williams had become the literary adviser for
the publishing firm of Smith, Elder and Company in 1845
and had responded enthusiastically to the manuscript of
Jane Eyre, which Charlotte Brontë had forwarded to the
firm in late August 1847. The novel was published on 16
October and was greeted with immediate success. *Wuthering
Heights, Agnes Grey* and *The Professor* had been rejected six
times before Thomas Cautley Newby accepted the first two
in July 1847 for publication as a three-volume set. In her 1850
'Biographical Notice of Ellis and Acton Bell', Charlotte
recalled that the manuscripts had been 'perseveringly
obtruded upon various publishers for the space of a year
and a half' concluding that 'their fate was an ignominious
and abrupt dismissal'. Newby accepted the two novels on
the condition that the authors contributed to the publishing
costs but even with this proviso having been accepted the
whole process of final publication took 5 months during
which time *Jane Eyre* had been both accepted and printed
by Smith, Elder and Company. It may well have been the
immediate success of Currer Bell's novel that prompted
Newby into finally producing *Wuthering Heights* and *Agnes
Grey* by Ellis and Acton Bell in December. Charlotte's comments to Williams in a letter of 21 December 1847 register
her great dissatisfaction at the presentation of the Newby
publications:

The orthography and punctuation of the books are
mortifying to a degree: almost all the errors that were

corrected in the proof-sheets appear intact in what should have been the fair copies. If Mr Newby always does business in this way, few authors would like to have him for their publisher a second time. (*The Brontës* II, p. 165)

In the same letter, Charlotte extends her comments on her sister's style of writing in *Wuthering Heights*:

Ellis has a strong, original mind, full of strange though sombre power: when he writes poetry that power speaks in language at once condensed, elaborated and refined – but in prose it breaks forth in scenes which shock more than they attract – Ellis will improve, however, because he knows his defects. (ibid.)

These comments made by Charlotte echo her earlier epithets about the novel being 'vigorous' and 'original' made in her letter to Williams dated 14 December . In terms of the publishing history of *Wuthering Heights*, since there is no existing original manuscript, nor even extracts from it, all future editors have been faced with the choice of following either Thomas Newby's error-ridden first edition or Charlotte Brontë's considerably edited second edition of 1850. As Pauline Nestor puts it in her brief note on the textual history in her Penguin Classics edition of the novel, which is used for all the quotations in this guide:

Determined to make amends, Charlotte made considerable changes to the second edition of Emily's novel. However, she was not content simply to correct typographical errors. She also changed the paragraphing to eliminate the prevalence of short paragraphs, altered the punctuation, tending to regularize Emily's rather idiosyncratic style, and modified the rendering of Joseph's dialect in order to make it more comprehensible.

CONTEMPORARY REVIEWS

Quotations from the contemporary reviews of Wuthering Heights can all be found in Miriam Allott's *The Brontës: The Critical Heritage.*

The first reviews of the novel highlighted incidents which 'are too coarse and disagreeable to be attractive' (*Spectator*, 18 December 1847) and commented on a dreariness 'so gloomy as the one here elaborated with such dismal minuteness' (*Athenaeum*, 25 December). The earliest of the five reviews which were discovered to have been kept by Emily in her desk is from *Examiner*, January 1848, and it not only refers to a Byronic influence on the writing of the novel, quoting a line from the 1814 poem, 'The Corsair', but also concentrates upon the character of Heathcliff in terms of 'implacable hate, ingratitude, cruelty, falsehood, selfishness, and revenge'. Interestingly, the unsigned review which appeared in *Britannia* on 15 January recognized that the violence found in this character was not confined to him alone and suggested that the novel 'would have been a far better romance if Heathcliff alone had been a being of stormy passions, instead of all the other characters being nearly as violent and destructive as himself'. It was this reviewer who associated the writing of the novel with the paintings of Salvator Rosa and commented on the 'impetuous force' of the narrative, 'the force of a dark and sullen torrent, flowing between high and rugged rocks', emphasizing the central role taken by landscape in this tale of 'passionate ferocity'.

The second edition of the novel was published by Smith and Elder on 7 December 1850 some 2 years after Emily's death and was accompanied by Charlotte's preface as Editor. She sent a copy of the book to Sydney Dobell in recognition of the belated but strikingly positive review he had published in Palladium 3 months earlier, where he had recognized the connection between the prose and landscape painting in his comment about 'a world of brilliant figures in an atmosphere of mist; shapes that come out upon the eye, and burn their colours into the brain, and depart into the enveloping fog'. Charlotte's *Preface* emphasizes from the start the rustic quality of the novel:

> It is Moorish, and wild, and knotty as a root of heath. Nor was it natural that it should be otherwise; the author being herself a native and nursling of the moors.

She recognizes the inextricable manner in which her sister's life had been bound up with the natural surroundings of the moors:

> Ellis Bell did not describe as one whose eye and taste alone found pleasure in the prospect; her native hills were far more to her than a spectacle; they were what she lived in, and by, as much as the wild birds, their tenants, or as the heather, their produce.

In the *Preface*, however, Charlotte also emphasizes the solitary and reclusive nature of her sister whose separation from the society of Haworth 'fostered her tendency to seclusion':

> Though her feeling for the people round was benevolent, intercourse with them she never sought; nor, with very few exceptions, ever experienced.

One result of this hermitic existence was to base her story on those 'tragic and terrible traits of which, in listening to the secret annals of every rude vicinage, the memory is sometimes compelled to receive the impress'. Therefore, suggesting that Emily's experience of human contact was often limited to the tales told of family histories and that her imagination 'was a spirit more sombre than sunny, more powerful than sportive' she 'wrought creations like Heathcliff, like Earnshaw, like Catherine':

> Having formed these beings, she did not know what she had done. If the auditor of her work when read in

CRITICAL RECEPTION AND PUBLISHING HISTORY

manuscript, shuddered under the grinding influence of natures so relentless and implacable, of spirits so lost and fallen; if it was complained that the mere hearing of certain vivid and fearful scenes banished sleep by night, and disturbed mental peace by day, Ellis Bell would wonder what was meant, and suspect the complainant of affectation.'

There is a strange form of apology here with the clear implication that if her sister had got out into society more, met more people and been more gregarious, then the brooding 'horror of great darkness', which informs the novel, would perhaps have been tempered by 'a mellower ripeness and sunnier bloom'. For Charlotte, the character of Heathcliff 'stands unredeemed'. His passionate love for Catherine Earnshaw 'is a sentiment fierce and inhuman: a passion such as might boil and glow in the bad essence of some evil genius', and his creation as a character is 'a man's shape animated by demon life – a Ghoul – an Alfreet'. This attitude towards Heathcliff bears out the comments made about her sister's reclusiveness in the letter Charlotte sent to W. S. Williams on 14 August 1848:

Heathcliff, again, of *Wuthering Heights* is quite another recreation. He exemplifies the effects which a life of continued injustice and hard usage may produce on a naturally perverse, vindictive, and inexorable disposition. Carefully trained and kindly treated, the black gipsy-cub might possibly have been reared into a human being, but tyranny and ignorance made of him a mere demon. The worst of it is, some of his spirit seems breathed through the whole narrative in which he figures: it haunts every moor and glen, and beckons in every fir-tree of the Heights.

It is almost as if Heathcliff is seen as a creation stemming from a mixture of Emily's reclusiveness and her fictive character's orphaned and socially deprived background. This type of excuse making, however, takes no real account of the commanding power of Emily Brontë's creation of Heathcliff, and it is worth bearing in mind the comments about the character of Shakespeare's Macbeth made by Wilbur Sanders in his essay 'What's Done, Is Done' in *Shakespeare's Magnanimity*:

> He is presented to us with that commanding mastery, which creates, by assuming, a human centrality for its subject.

Sanders points out that any logical account of Shakespeare's murderer ignores the 'kind of criminality' in which 'the notion of a cure is an impertinence':

Try (if you doubt it) to imagine a 'healthy' Macbeth – one who is able to rest in the impeccable logic of

> If chance will have me king,
> Why chance may crown me,
> Without my stir.

A Macbeth who, having answered his wife's persuasions with

> I dare do all that may become a man,
> Who dares do more, is none

(a complete answer!), firmly declines further argument, and amuses himself thereafter with occasional sallies from Cawdor Castle to unseam a passing Norwegian; who becomes a loyal and trusted liegeman to the boy Malcolm, when he succeeds to the throne; is to be seen at his own fireside on winter evenings, deep in conference with his old battle-comrade Banquo, with whom he enjoys metaphysical discussions on dreams and prophecies, free-will and necessity, spiced with reminiscences about witches of their acquaintance; until at a ripe old age he is elected to the throne (Malcolm having died of the combined avarice, gluttony and lechery he had promised to disclose once in power). I'm not just being facetious. Isn't it impossible (a) to feel that this calmly rational accommodation is available in the world we're shown? and (b) to pretend that it would be half as grand and gripping as what we are shown? This Macbeth would be so much less the man. (Sanders p. 59)

Given the power of Emily Brontë's creation of Heathcliff, it is no wonder that her sister should conclude the 1850 *Preface* with the statement:

Whether it is right or advisable to create beings like Heathcliff, I do not know: I scarcely think it is.

The *Leader* review of 28 December 1850, written by G. H. Lewes, brings to the fore this powerful and compelling nature of Heathcliff's character:

The power, indeed, is wonderful. Heathcliff, devil though he may be, is drawn with a sort of dusky splendour which fascinates, and we feel the truth of his burning and impassioned love for Catherine, and of her inextinguishable love for him. It was a happy thought to make her love the kind, weal, elegant Edgar, and yet without lessening her passion for Heathcliff. Edgar appeals to her love of refinement, and goodness, and culture; Heathcliff clutches her soul in his passionate embrace. Edgar is the husband she has chosen, the man who alone is fit to call her wife; but although she is ashamed of her early playmate she loves him with a passionate abandonment which sets culture, education, the world, at defiance.

Lewes was an intelligent and cultured reader, and the unsigned comments from *Eclectic Review* of February 1851 strike the more prevalent note of criticism about the character of Heathcliff by calling him 'a perfect monster, more demon than human', ending on a refusal to accept that Ellis Bell's characters exist in more than nightmare:

> They are devoid of truthfulness, are not in harmony with the actual world, and have, therefore, but little more power to move our sympathies than the romances of the middle ages, or the ghost stories which made our grand-dames tremble.

The central importance of Charlotte Brontë's *Preface* was highlighted by Philip Drew in his 'Charlotte Brontë as a Critic Of *Wuthering Heights*' (*Nineteenth-Century Fiction*, XVIII, no. 4 1964 p. 365 – 81) when he noted that 'the points she makes in her preface to the edition of 1850 are so different from those which trouble modern critics that they are worth careful attention on their own account, to say nothing of their unique value as the comments of an intelligent and informed contemporary, who was peculiarly well placed to understand the nature of the authoress's achievement':

> Her assessment of Heathcliff depends on a recognition of his superhuman villainy, whereas modern critics, if they move away from a consideration of the book's mechanism to a consideration of the moral relations of the characters, usually choose to minimize or justify Heathcliff's consistent delight in malice in order to elevate him to the status of hero.

The 'unredeemed' figure portrayed by Charlotte, 'never once swerving in his arrow-straight course to perdition' is seen by Drew against a particular literary background of those characters 'who are fated to work out their doom in torment and despair, characters such as Satan himself, Marlowe's Faustus and Mephistopheles, the Wandering Jew, Vanderdecken, or even Captain Ahab':

> It does not lead us to approve of Heathcliff's actions or even to condone them. Emily Brontë's achievement is to

arouse our sympathy for a lost soul while making it quite clear that his actions are damnable.

MORE RECENT CRITICAL ANALYSIS

Wuthering Heights has continued to attract a considerable amount of critical attention, and a comprehensive list of different approaches to the text can be found in the last chapter of this book dealing with Further Reading. In order to illustrate the range of engagement that has taken place, there are examples below of the work of three different influential critics in addition to an extract from C. P. Sanger's 1926 'The Structure of Wuthering Heights' with its chronological chart of the events within the novel.

1. An Introduction to the English Novel by Arnold Kettle, 1951

Wuthering Heights is about England in 1847 and the years before. The people it reveals live not in a never-never land but in Yorkshire. Heathcliff was born not in the pages of Byron, but in a Liverpool slum. The language of Nelly, Joseph and Hareton is the language of Yorkshire people. The story of *Wuthering Heights* is concerned not with love in the abstract, but with the passions of living people, with property-ownership, the attraction of social comforts, the arrangement of marriages, the importance of education, the validity of religion and the relations of rich and poor.

There is nothing vague about this novel; the mists in it are the mists of the Yorkshire moors; if we speak of it as having an elemental quality it is because the very elements, the great forces of nature are evoked, which change so slowly that in the span of a human life they seem unchanging. But in this evocation there is nothing sloppy or uncontrolled. On the contrary the realisation is intensely concrete: we seem to smell the kitchen of Wuthering Heights, to feel the force of the wind across the moors, to sense the very changes of the seasons. Such concreteness is achieved not by mistiness but by precision. (Kettle p. 131)

Arnold Kettle reminds us here that the writing in *Wuthering Heights* has a concrete reality to it, a sense of place and characterization that is firmly believable. However, he goes on to point out that the 'power and wonder' of the novel 'does not lie in naturalistic description, nor in a detailed analysis of the hour-by-hour issues of social living'. Kettle sees the novel as a symbolic representation of the class system of nineteenth-century England, what he refers to as 'a vision of what life in 1847 was like'. He sees the relationship between Catherine and Heathcliff as forged by their mutual feelings of rebellion against injustice, which starts as Heathcliff, 'the waif from the Liverpool slums', who had been treated kindly by old Earnshaw, is 'insulted and degraded by Hindley'. He highlights the revenge which Heathcliff takes against the whole family of Earnshaws and Lintons as having 'moral force' while at the same time being 'cruel and inhuman beyond normal thought'. Kettle suggests that although we cannot either admire or defend Heathcliff's position in the later stages of the novel, we do continue to sympathize with him and that it is Emily Brontë's achievement that she allows this to be the case:

> Heathcliff's revenge may involve a pathological condition of hatred, but it is not at bottom merely neurotic. It has a moral force. For what Heathcliff does is to use against his enemies with complete ruthlessness their own weapons, to turn on them (stripped of their romantic veils) their own standards, to beat them at their own game. The weapons he uses against the Earnshaws and Lintons are their own weapons of money and arranged marriages. He gets power over them by the classic methods of the ruling class, expropriation and property deals. (ibid. p. 139)

Our sympathy as readers is for Heathcliff because 'we recognize a rough moral justice in what he has done to his oppressors and because, though he is inhuman, we understand *why* he is inhuman.' His conclusion points to the power of this novel's imaginative understanding of social stresses and tensions:

> *Wuthering Heights* then is an expression in the imaginative terms of art of the stresses and tensions and conflicts, personal and spiritual, of nineteenth-century capitalist society. It is a novel without idealism, without false comforts, without any implication that power over their destinies rests outside the struggles and actions of human beings themselves. (ibid. p. 144)

2. 'A Fresh Approach to *Wuthering Heights*' by Q. D. Leavis, 1969

In her wide-ranging approach to reading the novel, a reading that includes a striking comparison with Henri-Pierre Roche's 1953 novel *Jules et Jim* and the film made of it by Francois Truffaut, Q. D. Leavis examines the Romantics' image of childhood in conflict with society and suggests that Emily Brontë gave the theme 'a new insight, and also a specific and informed sociological content':

> The theme is here very firmly rooted in time and place and richly documented: we cannot forget that Gimmerton and the neighbourhood are so bleak that the oats are always green there three weeks later than anywhere else, and that old Joseph's Puritan preachings accompany his 'overlaying his large Bible with dirty bank-notes, the produce of the day's transactions' at market; and we have a thoroughly realistic account of the life indoors and outdoors at Wuthering Heights as well as at the gentleman's residence at the Grange. (Leavis p. 98)

Leavis notes that the time scheme of the novel is such as 'to fix its happenings at a time when the old rough farming culture based on a naturally patriarchal family life, was to be challenged, tamed and routed by social and cultural challenges that were to produce the Victorian class consciousness and 'unnatural' ideal of gentility' (p. 99). She points to the opposition between the Heights and Thrushcross Grange as being a clash of 'two different cultures of which the latter inevitably supersedes the former' (p. 99) and highlights the differences between the two worlds:

> The corresponding differences between the farm-house culture of Wuthering Heights and the polite world of Thrushcross Grange in social attitudes, instinctive behaviour, physical appearance and health, style of speech, way of living, dress, deportment, emotional habits – the whole idiom of life – are perpetually kept before us and are given their due importance in determining action, plot and characterization. Even the difference between both these orders and the fashionable society of city and watering-place from which Lockwood takes his tone, is never forgotten (brought out afresh at the opening of II, XVIII when Lockwood pays his final visit to the Heights). Isabella's illusions which lead to her wretched marriage are as characteristic of the over-sheltered life at the Grange as the lung-disease from which all the Lintons die except Catherine's daughter (who is half an Earnshaw). The importance of the sociological content of the novel to the novelist is proved by her pains to show Heathcliff's eventual regrets about his enemies' son Hareton, only because Hareton's wounded feelings (due to the position Heathcliff has deliberately placed him in) remind him of his own embittered youth as the uncouth ploughboy; he never softens to Cathy, the child of his other enemy, though she is also the daughter of his beloved Catherine and had suffered more at his hands than Hareton. (ibid. p. 121)

Leavis's clear sense of respect for the rural community represented by the Heights comes out most strongly when she

CRITICAL RECEPTION AND PUBLISHING HISTORY

refers to the fruit bushes that have been uprooted to make
way for a flower garden:

> Similarly, when Cathy in her thoughtlessness uses her
> new power over Hareton to get him to pull up the fruit-
> bushes to make her a flower-garden, old Joseph, who
> has worked all his life at the Heights and meant to die
> there, is so outraged that he gives notice rather than
> stay to witness such a sinful proceeding as to sacri-
> fice food to flowers. Unattractive as Joseph usually is,
> his disinterested identification with the family's well-
> being is impressive and as so often he is the vehicle for
> expressing a truth to which we need to have our atten-
> tion called: here, that where fertile soil is precious,
> flower-gardens are an unjustified self-indulgence. (ibid.
> p. 103)

3. 'Changing the Names: The Two Catherines' by Lyn Pykett 1989

Concentrating upon the choices made by Catherine
Earnshaw and their consequences, Lyn Pykett brings into
question what she terms 'the fictional paradigm which struc-
tures a woman's life as a choice between two men'. Pykett
points to the choosing of an appropriate husband as being
one of the central moral tasks facing the heroine of most
eighteenth- and nineteenth-century novels:

> However, *Wuthering Heights* departs from fictional and
> social norms by exploring the consequences of the socially
> sanctioned choice. In Catherine's case, marriage is not
> the answer to the problem of her life, the resolver of all
> contradictions, as it usually is in domestic and romantic
> fiction. On the contrary, marriage compounds the prob-
> lems of Catherine's life and exposes its contradictions.
> The return of Heathcliff in the later stages of Catherine's
> story exposes the inadequacies of an apparently appropri-
> ate marriage, and raises questions about both the nature

of the choice Catherine had been required to make and the capacity of genteel marriage to comprehend all of a woman's needs.

As Pykett points out, the young Catherine, brought up motherless and subsequently fatherless in an isolated part of the country, 'reaches puberty relatively untrammelled by parental notions of suitable feminine conduct'. As a consequence of this, her transformation into a young lady who will fit in to the socially acceptable world of the Grange is seen as a significant sense of loss. This idea of Catherine's fall from one world to another is also interestingly central to the seminal study of women writers in the nineteenth century, *The Madwoman in the Attic* by Sandra M. Gilbert and Susan Gubar. Pykett links Catherine's marriage to a fall from which she can only yearn to recover:

> The adult Catherine persistently yearns for the self-consistency of the girlhood state that pre-existed the self-divisions induced by her education into the class-gender role of the genteel lady.

Although the figure of Catherine may be seen as a powerful one, Pykett argues that the power is only self-consuming because the whole story presents the reader with a clear dramatization of the limits of female power and influence in the society of mid nineteenth-century England:

> Her marriage to Edgar, which ironically she sees as a means of empowering herself to assist Heathcliff, proves unable to reconcile the two men, and her belief in the power of her influence over Heathcliff is equally illusory. In short, Catherine's story vividly illustrates the fact that no matter how powerful and ruling her personality, a woman, as defined in nineteenth-century ideologies of gender and the family, must always cede definition and

control to others and she is always, at least potentially, a victim. The spirited and rebellious Catherine must ultimately submit to the legal control of her father, her brother, and subsequently her husband. As she passes from childhood she becomes the victim of the ideal of feminine gentility. She also becomes the object of a competitive struggle between two men, each of whom wants her to conform to his own version of her.

Pykett looks at the second-generation Catherine as both a repetition and a variant of the first:

In some senses Cathy's story reverses rather than repeats her mother's. For example, whereas the first Catherine's puberty is marked by a rite of passage from the Heights to the Grange, and from rebellious childhood to constrainedly genteel adolescence, her daughter makes the journey in reverse. Cathy's first acquaintance with the Heights, like her mother's with the Grange, is the result of an act of curiosity and rebellion which has misfired. Cathy finds herself at the Heights after illicitly attempting to reach the enchanted and forbidden territory of Penistone Crags, whose 'golden rocks' have hitherto marked the physical limits of her horizon and the boundary of her childhood obedience.

Pursuing her comparison between the two female figures, Pykett concludes that Cathy is capable of achieving what is beyond the power of her mother:

Having learned to divest herself of many of the forms of feminine gentility, Cathy reconstructs both herself and Hareton. Whereas Catherine is destroyed by her inability to reconcile conflicting images of herself and the contradictory definitions of the feminine which confront her, Cathy negotiates them and ultimately constructs a new role for herself.

4. The Chronology of Wuthering Heights by C. P. Sanger

Volume I Chapter			
	1757	before September	birth of Hindley Earnshaw
	1762	"	birth of Edgar Linton
	1764	"	birth of Heathcliff
	1765	Summer	birth of Catherine Earnshaw
	1765	Late	birth of Isabella Linton
IV	1771	Summer, beginning of harvest	Heathcliff brought to Wuthering Heights
	1773	Spring or early summer	Mrs. Earnshaw dies
V	1774	October	Hindley sent to college
	1777		Hindley marries
	"	"	Mr. Earnshaw dies
VI	"	"	Hindley returns with his wife
III	"	October or November	The scene described by Catherine

VI	"	November, third week, Sunday	Catherine and Heathcliff go to Thrushcross Grange
VII	1777	Christmas Eve	Catherine returns to Wuthering Heights
	"	Christmas Day	The Lintons visit Wuthering Heights
VIII	1778	June	Hareton Earnshaw born
	"	Late	Frances Earnshaw dies
	1780	Summer	Edgar Linton calls at Wuthering Heights and proposes to Catherine
IX	"	"	Hindley returns drunk
	"	"	Catherine tells Ellen about Edgar
	"	"	Heathcliff goes off
	"	"	Catherine gets wet through and catches fever

	"	Autumn	Catherine, convalescent, goes to Thrushcross Grange. Mr. and Mrs. Linton catch the fever and die
	1783	April	Edgar marries Catherine
X	"	September	Heathcliff returns and sees Catherine
	"	Autumn	Isabella falls in love with Heathcliff, who visits Thrushcross Grange from time to time
XI	"	December	Ellen Dean sees Hareton. Heathcliff kisses Isabella
	1784	6 January, Monday	Violent scene at Thrushcross Grange. Heathcliff is turned out and Catherine goes on hunger strike

XII	"	10 January, Friday	Catherine delirious
	"	2 a.m.	Isabella elopes with Heathcliff
XIII	"	13 March, Monday	The Heathcliff's return to Wuthering Heights
XIV	"	15 March, Wednesday	Ellen Dean goes to Wuthering Heights
Volume 2 I	"	19 March, Sunday	Heathcliff sees Catherine: violent scene
II	"	"midnight	Catherine Linton born
	"	20 March , Monday, 2 a.m.	Catherine (the elder) dies
	"	21 March, Tuesday	Heathcliff puts a lock of hair in Catherine's locket
	"	24 March, Friday	Catherine's funeral
III	"	Same day, midnight	Heathcliff nearly kills Hindley, who tried to kill him
		25 March, Saturday	Isabella runs off

	"	September	Linton Heathcliff born
	"	September or October	Hindley Earnshaw dies. All his property is mortgaged to Heathcliff
IV	1797	Early June	Catherine goes to Penistone Crags and meets Hareton
V	"	June	Isabella dies. Edgar brings back Linton Heathcliff
VI	"	"	Linton Heathcliff is taken to live at Wuthering Heights
VII	1800	20 March	Catherine and Ellen meet Hareton and go to Wuthering Heights where they see Linton
	"	March or April	Catherine and Linton correspond
VIII	"	Late October or November	Catherine sees Heathcliff, who says that Linton is seriously ill

XIX	"	Late October or November	Catherine and Ellen go to see Linton. Ellen catches cold and is ill for 3 weeks
X	"	November	During Ellen's illness, Catherine visits Linton secretly
XI	1801	20 March	Edgar too ill to visit his wife's grave
	"	June	Edgar declining
XII	"	August	Ellen and Catherine go to meet Linton
	"	August, Thursday, a week later	They are kidnapped
	"	Monday?	Catherine and Linton marry
XIII	"	August or September	Ellen is let out
		Next Tuesday	Edgar is dying; he sends for Mr. Green, the lawyer, who does not come

	"	Harvest moon	Catherine escapes and comes to Thrushcross Grange
XIV	"	Wednesday, 3 a.m.	Edgar Linton dies
XV	"	September, evening after the funeral	Heathcliff comes to the Grange and takes off Catherine
XVI	"	October	Linton Heathcliff dies. Hareton tries to please Catherine
Volume II	"	Late November	Lockwood calls at Wuthering Heights
II	"	Next day	He calls again and has to stay the night. He finds Catherine's diary and sees Heathcliff's outburst
	"	Next day	Leaves at eight. Catches cold.
IV	"	"	Ellen Dean begins her story

X	"	3 weeks later	Heathcliff sends grouse
	"	1 week later	Heathcliff calls
Volume III	1802	January, 1 week later	Lockwood continues his account
XVII	"	January, second week	Lockwood calls at Wuthering Heights
XVIII	"	Beginning of February	Ellen goes to live at Wuthering Heights
	"	March	Hareton has an accident
	"	Easter Monday	Catherine is nice to Hareton
XIX	"	Easter Tuesday	Scene about altering garden
	"	(After March 18)	Heathcliff getting odd
XX	"	April	Heathcliff goes on hunger strike
	"	May	Heathcliff dies

	September	Lockwood visits Thrushcross Grange and Wuthering Heights
1803	1 January	Catherine and Hareton marry

STUDY QUESTIONS

1. In his essay 'Control of Sympathy in *Wuthering Heights*', John Hagan writes: 'One of Emily Brontë's major achievements in *Wuthering Heights* is to keep alive the reader's sympathy for both Catherine and Heathcliff, even though their behaviour after the former's marriage to Edgar Linton becomes increasingly bizarre and frightening akin to the demonic.' How true do you find this in your reading of the novel? You may find it interesting to compare this with the way your sympathies are both retained and withheld from the characters of Jane and Rochester in *Jane Eyre*.

2. Editors of *Wuthering Heights* nowadays tend to use the first edition of the novel rather than Charlotte Brontë's emended 1850 edition as the basis from which to start. How much do you feel is lost by the standardization of dialogue and spelling which Charlotte felt necessary for the British public?

CHAPTER 5

ADAPTATION, INTERPRETATION AND INFLUENCE

The distinguished six-reel silent film of *Wuthering Heights* was directed by the English actor – director A. V. Bramble for the Ideal Film Renting Company in 1920, and the location chosen was Haworth. Interestingly, the Brontë Society was thoroughly co-operative, and there was a considerable care taken over the authenticity of the details in this version. The account given of the film in *The Oxford Companion to the Brontës* is clear in its judgement of this early version:

> Three actors were used for Heathcliff, and two for Hindley and Edgar, to make sure that they 'grew up' convincingly. Even more surprising, given that the film lasted no more than an hour and a half, was the fact that all the second-generation characters were included, and that Hareton and the second generation Catherine also had child and adult versions. The adult Heathcliff and Catherine were played by Milton Rosmer and Anne Trevor. The gestures of the actors resemble those of the Victorian stage melodrama, but the dramatic still of Catherine's death scene combines heightened gestures with realistic indications of her illness. (Alexander and Smith p. 193)

The billing of the film as 'Emily Brontë's tremendous Story of Hate' placed one particular emphasis on the plot line, and a member of the Brontë Society commented at the time that 'the more gruesome elements of the story have been minimised' so that the film could obtain its 'A' certificate. As if in a strange form of counterpart to the manuscript of the novel, there is no surviving copy of the film.

The 1939 Samuel Goldwyn film directed by William Wyler has become one of the defining film versions of the novel despite the enormous liberties it took with the text of the story. Laurence Olivier was cast as Heathcliff, and he wanted his future wife Vivien Leigh to play the part of Catherine. However, the studio executives decided that the part should be taken by Merle Oberon. The possibilities of Vivien Leigh being given the role highlight one prominent aspect of the film: its demand for an immediate comparison with its exact contemporary 'Gone With the Wind'. The passionate love between Heathcliff and Catherine and the fairytale land of Penistone Crag where they seem to discover a Utopian haven where true love can exist is remote from Emily Brontë's novel, and it is entirely in keeping with the film's aim that it should simply remove the second generation, cutting the book in half. Presumably, the idea of the thwarted true love between the hero and heroine, the Romantic immensity of a Romeo and Juliet style as 'star-crossed lovers', would be severely confused by the existence of children and by the far from Romantic behaviour of Heathcliff concerning property rights and entails. The role of Isabella in the film takes on a position of central power as she becomes a foil to Catherine who, in turn, is so distraught at the idea of her sister-in-law marrying Heathcliff that she begs Edgar to kill them both! As the doting Isabella clings to Heathcliff in their Heights home, he asks why there is no smell of heather in her hair as though her association with the socially successful Grange has meant that she is dislocated from the natural world of the moors. Heathcliff has married Edgar's sister as a simple act of spite against Catherine, and this accords more read-ily with the deeply unhappy rejected lover than the calcu-lating question about whether or not Isabella was Edgar's heir that he had asked Catherine in the novel. In Lin Haire-Sargeant's essay on the problem of filming Heathcliff, she comments on the 'psychologizing sympathy' expressed by Olivier as he shares his own sense of isolation with Isabella, telling her 'You're lonely... It's lonely sitting like an outsider in so happy a household as your bother's... You won't be lonely any more':

> On the page this is almost laughably far from Brontë's Heathcliff, but paradoxically, of all the Heathcliffs, the Wyler/Olivier version gives the strongest analog of Heathcliff's felt emotion, the injustices endured and absorbed, the repressed passion and rage. (Haire-Sargeant p. 167)

Similarly, the passionate way in which Isabella clings to her husband in the film is a world away from the quietly menacing threat of physical violence that Heathcliff communicates to Catherine in the book:

> You'd hear of odd things, if I lived alone with that mawkish, waxen face; the most ordinary would be painting on its white the colours of the rainbow, and turning the blue eyes black, every day or two; they detestably resemble Linton's.

As Olivier stares down into Geraldine Fitzgerald's eyes, he mournfully asks why her eyes are always empty like Linton's eyes, and we are left with the lingering sense of a tragic loss where the two lovers who have been socially parted will only ever find true togetherness in the afterlife. Interestingly, Goldwyn originally wanted the film's title changed from 'Wuthering Heights' to 'He Died for Her', which would clearly dictate the way the audience's sympathies were being directed:

> The character of Heathcliff is softened... and Catherine's is sharpened so that she appears as a coquettish social climber who loses interest in Heathcliff because of his inability to fulfil her ambitions. (ibid.)

This emphasis upon Catherine Earnshaw's social aspirations is taken further with the reference to Heathcliff having gone to America in order to make his money, and there are hints of the world of a character from Henry James: the self-made businessman who wishes to court the old European values but who is still regarded as an outsider!

> The plot is severely truncated to end with the death of the elder Catherine, which is elevated to tragic status by gestures toward the 'other-worldly' aspects of the novel. In particular, Penistone Crag serves throughout the film as a lovers' tryst, where Catherine declares that she wants 'everything to stop' so that they can be frozen in their youthful togetherness. Developed into a filmic motif, a snowbound Peniston Crag becomes the site of Heathcliff's death and of his ghostly reunion with Catherine. (ibid.)

Accompanied by Alfred Newman's music, which again provided a clear counterpart to Max Steiner's score for 'Gone with the Wind', the film ends with the ghostly figures of the dead Catherine and Heathcliff walking hand in hand through the snows-cape up towards their spiritual home under Penistone Crag. The openness of the landscape serves as a convincing contrast to the claustrophobic and glittering world of the Grange with its balls and music reflected in the pent-up dress of the social milieu. As Dr. Kenneth asks Flora Robson's Ellen at the end of the film whether the two thwarted lovers are just both dead, she replies, staring beatifically into the distance:

> No! They've just begun to live!

The startling contrast between this and the end of Emily Brontë's unsettling novel is clearly felt in Ellen's comments:

> But the country folks, if you asked them, would swear on their Bible that he *walks*. There are those who speak to having met him near the church, and on the moor, and even within this house – Idle tales, you'll say, and so say I. Yet that old man by the kitchen fire affirms he has seen

two on 'em, looking out of his chamber window, on every
rainy night, since his death. (p. 333)

The use of the emphasized word 'walks' adds to the dis-
comfort of a haunting disquiet, and the vengeful figure of
the lone Heathcliff seen in various parts suggests nothing
of the film's loving peace and mutual happiness. The novel
does not end with a sense of escape, and it is worth com-
paring Lockwood's rather banal closing paragraph with
Ellen's more uncomfortable sense that has echoes of the
world of *Macbeth*. Lockwood closes his narrative with the
sense of a man who has closed up the book he has read
with a sentimental sigh of satisfaction:

I sought, and soon discovered, the three head-stones on
the slope next the moor – the middle one, grey, and half
buried in heath – Edgar Linton's only harmonized by
the turf, and moss creeping up its foot – Heathcliff's still
bare.
  I lingered round them, under that benign sky; watched
the moths fluttering among the heath, and hare-bells; listened to the soft wind breathing through the grass; and
wondered how any one could ever imagine unquiet slumbers, for the sleepers in that quiet earth. (p. 334)

The reference here to Heathcliff's grave being 'still bare'
only conveys the newness of the freshly dug grave rather
than any sense of bleakness, and the sound of 'soft wind'
allows the potentially uncomfortable word 'breathing' to be
dissolved so that sleep will not be disturbed.
  By contrast, Ellen's closing words on the previous page
leave one with a distinctly less soothing feeling, and it is
worth recalling that these are the words of the person whose
narrative has dominated the book:

...yet still, I don't like being out in the dark, now – and
I don't like being left by myself in this grim house – I

cannot help it, I shall be glad when they leave it, and shift to the Grange!

This nervousness is closer to Shakespeare's sense of the darkness, which makes the first murderer in Macbeth say:

The west yet glimmers with some streaks of day.
Now spurs the lated traveler apace
To gain the timely inn...
(Act III, scene III, 5–7)

The possibility of Heathcliff's resurrection is closer to Macbeth's horror as he recognizes that

The time has been
That, when the brains were out, the man would die,
And there an end.
(Act III, scene IV, 77–9)

It is this sense of haunting horror which bursts out of Fritz Eichenberg's wood engravings, which illustrated the Random House Modern Library edition of the novel in 1943. In particular, the picture of Heathcliff digging up Catherine's grave has a ghoulish sense of the grave robber who is being caught in the act, while the earlier scene of Lockwood's dream gives the sense of a man in the throes of a nightmare who is brandishing a severed arm which has been thrust through the broken window.

A Japanese interpretation of the story, *Onimaru*, was directed by Yoshige Yoshida in 1988, with Yuko Tanaka as the Catherine figure and Yusaku Matsuda as an inarticulate warrior Heathcliff. Here, the novel is transposed to a medieval Japan, but the atmosphere of brooding vengeance accords with the underlying theme of the novel: the destabilizing effects of unrequited and isolated love. In *Onimaru*, an outcast boy is adopted by a family of priests, but like young Heathcliff, he threatens the established hierarchy and acts in defiance of what are perceived as the ancient local and social rites. Onimaru is in love with Kinu who in turn weds the heir to a rival family in order to avoid her fate of being made into a priestess. The rejected Onimaru isolates himself as a figure of outcast splendour, Lord of the Mountain, and indulges himself in a style of cruelty, the intensity of which matches the strength of his thwarted love. The undercurrent of incest and violence suggests a type of unstoppable natural force.

Another of the interesting comparisons that has been made between Emily Brontë's text and the world of film was put forward by Q. D. Leavis in her 1966 lectures in America, 'A Fresh Approach to *Wuthering Heights*'. Here, she suggests an intriguing connection between the substance of the nineteenth-century novel and the film *Jules et Jim*, made in 1962 by Francois Truffaut, which was based upon the earlier novel of the same name by Henri-Pierre Roche. The theme of both the film and its source is the woman who is loved by two very different men. Charlotte Bronte had referred to 'the perverted passion and passionate perversity' of Catherine Earnshaw, and Leavis takes up this point:

Kate answers exactly to Charlotte Bronte's description above of Catherine Earnshaw as well as in nearly all other essentials – it seems not to matter that, living in a sexually permissive society (twentieth-century Germany and France) she takes full licence, for she ends in Catherine's situation, and endures and causes similar suffering. Jules whom she marries is gentle, with bookish and philosophic leanings, like Edgar Linton, while Jim, a write, is passionate, hard and violent, providing for Kate something that she needs to keep her alive and whole that her husband lacks – though she can't do without what Jules stands for either. Acquiescent as Jules inevitably is, considering the sophisticated society in which they live, and even by choice since his deep friendship with Jim antedates their meeting with Kate, and also because he hopes that, Jim being for Kate a lover who supplements himself in temperament, his marriage will be saved (he has two little girls) – yet the situation is inherently disastrous and ends with Kate's destroying herself and dragging the not unwilling Jim with her, while Jules survives, like Edgar Linton, only to foster his little daughters. (Leavis p. 105)

The idyllic moments which haunt the film are juxtaposed with an atmosphere of approaching doom, and Jeanne Moreau's central role as the torn Catherine conveys a sense of an extraordinary woman whose gaiety and charm are inseparable from her determined needs for self-satisfaction. The film is set against a background of war where Jules and Jim are fighting on opposite sides, and it ends with the suicide of Catherine and Jim leaving us with the sense of love and death being inextricably wound together.

The interweaving of the theme of love and death is central to Luis Bunuel's black-and-white version of the story made in 1953, 'Abismos de Pasion', where the director opens his film with the statement:

These characters are at the mercy of their own instincts and passions. They are unique beings for whom the so-called social conventions do not exist. Alejandro's love for Catalina is a fierce and inhuman feeling that can only be fulfilled through death.

Buñuel had revealed an interest in filming the tale of Heathcliff and Cathy as thwarted lovers for some 20 years before the making of this version, which is set in the hacienda world of Mexico. The film may well have been inspired by Georges Bataille's book, *Literature and Evil* (1957), in which he includes an appraisal of *Wuthering Heights*, and in the interview which Bataille gave in the following year, he concentrated upon the interwoven aspects of the act of fictional writing and a notion of evil, which casts an interesting light on the role of Heathcliff. In his notes for the New York State Writers Institute Kevin

Jack Hagopian, Senior Lecturer in Media Studies at Pennsylvania State University highlights the fascination of the story for Buñuel:

What fascinated Buñuel about the novel was its portrait of *l'amour fou*, mad love, the self-immolating passion that sweeps reason before it in a hurricane of jealousy and doubt. This kind of love revealed the lies and hypocrisies of the world, as the lovers' desire for one another tears away social artifice and convention, leaving only the raw fact of human desire. Buñuel not only understood the power of this kind of love, he reveled in it as the only pure force available in a world of willful deception, writing in a 1929 question on surrealism that "I would willingly sacrifice my liberty to love." Indeed, many of Buñuel's films over the next decades after making that statement deal with the willing exchange of liberty for love, culminating in his 1965 masterwork of love suborned by obsession, *Belle de Jour*. *Wuthering Heights*, in particular, with its incipient themes of marriage for economic gain and the explosive ability of a soul in love to deny reality and compulsively harm itself and others, made *Wuthering Heights*, for Buñuel, not a watery-eyed romance novel, but the story of a tempest of rage and self-indulgence which ranges over a landscape of class and sexual taboos, leaving devastation in its wake. Buñuel watches approvingly as passion fulfills itself at any cost, following its own logic, charting its own deadly course.

With the Paramount version of the novel directed by Peter Kosminsky in 1992, the filming was returned to the moorlands surrounding Haworth, and the photography is stunning. The brooding atmosphere is dominated by a Wuthering Heights that is more castellated fortification than farmhouse, and here, there is a clear reference to the possibility of High Sunderland Hall near Halifax being the original for Emily's Heights rather than the low farmhouse of Top

Withens. High Sunderland Hall was inhabited by tenant farmers at the time that Emily was teaching not far away at Law Hill, and she would certainly have known of its façade of carvings over the door and gateway. A grotesque head formed the keystone to the arch of the gateway, while other heads with lewd faces seem to foreshadow the 'wilderness of crumbling griffins, and shameless little boys' that Lockwood notes as decorating the outside of the Heights. Ralph Fiennes presents us with a Heathcliff who has a cold and merciless sense, a vindictiveness which is all the more effective by being restrained. When he confronts Edgar in the kitchen and Catherine locks them in, there is the clear potential for explosive action. Here, Fiennes is the master of the quiet sneer, which has a menacing tone to it. However, when Edgar hits him and he in turn picks up a poker to strike the man down, Catherine clearly forbids him to do it and, without rushing Fiennes, uses the poker to smash the lock and leave. What we are left with is a disturbing feeling of pent-up aggression, which will find its outlet another way. Kosminsky's film was titled 'Emily Brontë's Wuthering Heights' not only because Sam Goldwyn held the rights to the title of the novel but also because it enabled him to introduce the author herself as a Romantic visitor to the ruined Heights. We are presented here with the process of dramatic creation as the Brontë figure tells us that 'My pen creates stories of a world that might have been, and here is one that I will tell.' Juliette Binoche plays the mesmerizing Catherine in both generations, and her face haunts the whole film from the very beginning when Lockwood arrives at the Heights to see her sitting white and stony-faced in the gloomy interior. One of the false feelings in the film is caused by the lack of understanding about the time scheme of the story. In the novel, Catherine and Heathcliff are 12 and 13 years old, respectively, when they rebel against the tedious religious sermons of the Calvinist Joseph, and they are seen in the novel as still being children. For instance, Lockwood reads the following account of life at the Heights

during the time between Hindley's return and the death of
Frances:

'An awful Sunday!' commenced the paragraph beneath.
'I wish my father were back again. Hindley is a detestable
substitute – his conduct to Heathcliff is atrocious – H.
and I are going to rebel – we took our initiatory step this
evening.

'All day had been flooding with rain; we could not go
to church, so Joseph must needs get up a congregation in
the garret; and, while Hindley and his wife basked down-
stairs before a comfortable fire – doing anything but reading their Bibles, I'll answer for it – Heathcliff, myself, and
the unhappy plough-boy, were commanded to take our
Prayer-books, and mount – we were ranged in a row, on
a sack of corn, groaning and shivering, and hoping that
Joseph would shiver too, so that he might give us a short
homily for his own sake. A vain idea! The service lasted
precisely three hours; and yet my brother had the face to
exclaim, when he saw us descending,

'"What, done already?"

'On Sunday evenings we used to be permitted to play,
if we did not make much noise; now a mere titter is sufficient to send us into corners!'. (p. 20–1)

The tone of this language creates a scene that would not be
amiss in a Phiz illustration for Dickens, and the use of
phrases like 'ranged in a row' conveys the harsh world of
Victorian rural schools. Lin Haire-Sargeant points force-
fully to the way in which Kosminsky's rendering of the early
years of Catherine and Heathcliff misses out the whole world
of childhood:

It is a fault of this version that it slides too quickly over
the shared childhood that grounds their love. Their early
paradisiacal relationship, young Cathy and Heathcliff
in Eden, should be established using plausible child

actors...but Kosminsky dispatches his youngsters in seconds. Instead, suddenly we are confronted with the undisguisably adult Binoche and Fiennes essaying kiddie roles. They giggle through a scripture lesson, then, reprimanded, scamper off to their shred bed to play (of all things!) a guessing game about flowers and trees. These scenes are so obviously wrong that their inclusion seems like wanton sabotage, but Kosminsky won't give screen time to peripheral actors. He wants to immediately drench us with the glorious light of his big stars, and he wants to keep us in that light without distraction. (Haire-Sargeant p. 423)

One of the most interesting artistic reactions to *Wuthering Heights* and its landscape comes from the American poet Sylvia Plath and her Yorkshire born husband Ted Hughes. While on a visit to the Hughes family home in Yorkshire in September 1956, Plath wrote to her mother:

There is no way to Wuthering Heights except by foot for several miles over the moors. How can I tell you how wonderful it is. Imagine yourself on top of the world, with all the purplish hills curving away, and gray sheep grazing with horns curling and black demonic faces and yellow eyes...black walls of stone, clear streams from which we drank; and, at last, a lonely, deserted blackstone house, broken down, clinging to the windy side of a hill. I began a sketch of the sagging roof and stone walls. (*Letters Home* p. 269)

The house referred to by Plath is Top Withens. Nine days later, Plath wrote again to her mother to tell her that she had just reread Emily Brontë's novel 'and really *felt* it this time more than ever.' Five years later, in September 1961, Plath wrote her poem 'Wuthering Heights', in which she goes some way to identifying herself with a trapped world of the moors. The poem opens with her as a witch-like figure tied to the stake for execution as 'The horizons ring me like faggots' and continues with a sense of the land drawing her in:

> There is no life higher than the grasstops
> Or the hearts of sheep, and the wind
> Pours by like destiny, bending
> Everything in one direction.
> I can feel it trying
> To funnel my heat away.
> If I pay the roots of the heather
> Too close attention, they will invite me
> To whiten my bones among them.

The immersion of personality within landscape is central to the images of *Wuthering Heights* where Heathcliff and Catherine lie side by side in the ground. With a shrewd critical insight, Plath recognizes how the image of windows and doors, ouvertures, allows for the passing of memory and emotion to and fro between the living and the dead:

> I come to wheel ruts, and water
> Limpid as the solitudes
> That flee through my fingers.
> Hollow doorsteps go from grass to grass;
> Lintel and sill have unhinged themselves.
> Of people the air only
> Remembers a few odd syllables.
> It rehearses them moaningly:
> Black stone, black stone.

Ted Hughes remembered the day vividly and wrote about it in 'Two Photographs of Top Withens' published in 1993. Hughes's awareness of the isolation and brooding threat of the landscape is caught with a frisson of horror:

> 'We could buy this place and renovate it!'
> Except, of course, except,

On second thoughts, maybe, except
For the empty horror of the moor –
Mad heather and grass tugged by the mad
And empty wind
That has petrified or got rid of
Everything but the stones.
The stones are safe, being stone.
Even the spirit of the place, like Emily's,
Hidden beneath stone.

In 'Wuthering Heights', a poem included in *Birthday Letters*, Hughes recalls the incident of that walk again and refers back to the idea of whether or not one could take up residence in this bleak landscape:

The incomings,
The outgoings – how would you take up now
The clench of that struggle? The leakage
Of earnings off a few sickly bullocks
And a scatter of crazed sheep. Being cornered
Kept folk here. Was that crumble of wall
Remembering a try at a garden? Two trees
Planted for company, for a child to play under,
And to have something to stare at. Sycamores –
The girth and spread of valley twenty-year-olds,
They were probably ninety.

More effectively that any film made of the novel, these images remind us of the difficulties of grubbing a living out of inhospitable land and bring home the grievance felt by Joseph at having the fruit trees pulled up to make way for a flower garden. When earning money can be seen in terms of 'leakage', it offers a new perspective on Joseph's placing 'dirty bank-notes' on his Bible, 'the produce of the day's transactions' (p. 312). Hughes also wrote 'Top Withens' as an accompanying poem to Fay Godwin's highly atmospheric photograph which was published in *Remains of Elmet, A Pennine Sequence*. Hughes's poem emphasizes 'the skylines, howling', while Godwin's black-and-white photograph presents the eye with a farmhouse which sits like a fortification on the hill top. Pursuing the associations between Sylvia Plath and Emily Brontë, two young women who began writing at a very young age and who would both be dead by the age of 30, Hughes refers to the author of *Wuthering Heights* as staring 'Like a dying prisoner', whereas Plath possessed a huge/Mortgage of hope':

> The moor-wind
> Came with its empty eyes to look at you,
> And the clouds gazed sidelong, going elsewhere,
> The heath-grass, fidgeting in its fever,
> Took idiot notice of you. And the stone,
> Reaching to touch your hand, found you real
> And warm, and lucent, like that earlier one.
> And maybe a ghost, trying to hear your words,
> Peered from the broken mullions
> And was stilled. Or was suddenly aflame
> With the scorch of doubled envy. Only
> Gradually quenched in understanding.

STUDY QUESTIONS

1. If you were making a new film version of *Wuthering Heights*, would you insist upon it being filmed in a topographical location on the Yorkshire Moors or would you want to bring out the enduring qualities of love and revenge in a different context?
2. How important do you think it is to include the second generation of characters in a film version of *Wuthering Heights*?
3. If you were to consider creating a stage adaptation of *Wuthering Heights*, you would have to leave out some of the scenes. Which scenes would you see as being central and therefore must be included?

CHAPTER 6

BIBLIOGRAPHY

EDITIONS OF *WUTHERING HEIGHTS*

Wuthering Heights, a novel by Ellis Bell in three volumes, London: Newby, 1847. This first edition contained *Wuthering Heights* in the first two volumes and *Agnes Grey* in the third.

Wuthering Heights, a new edition revised, with a biographical notice of the authors, a selection from their literary remains, and a preface by Currer Bell, London: Smith, Elder, 1850.

Wuthering Heights, ed. Hilda Marsden and Ian Jack, Oxford: Clarendon Press, 1976.

Wuthering Heights, ed. Pauline Nestor, Harmondsworth: Penguin Classics, 1995.

Oxford World's Classics, ed. Ian Jack, with introduction and notes by Patsy Stoneman, Oxford: Oxford University Press, 1998.

Wuthering Heights, ed. Richard J. Dunn, Norton Critical Edition (fourth edition), New York and London: W.W. Norton & Company, 2003.

Wuthering Heights, case studies in contemporary criticism, ed. Linda H. Peterson, Boston, MA: Bedford, 2003.

EDITIONS OF EMILY BRONTË'S POETRY

The Complete Poems of Emily Jane Brontë, ed. C.W. Hatfield, New York: Columbia University Press, 1941.

The Brontës: Selected Poems, ed. Juliet Barker, London: Dent, 1985.

Emily Jane Brontë: The Complete Poems, ed. Janet Gezari, Harmonsworth: Penguin, 1992.

The Poems of Emily Brontë, ed. Derek Roper and Edward Chitham, Oxford: Oxford University Press, 1994.

OTHER WORKS BY THE BRONTËS

Agnes Grey by Anne Brontë, edited with an introduction and notes by Angeline Goreau, Harmondsworth: Penguin, 1988.

The Professor by Charlotte Brontë, ed. Heather Glen, Harmondsworth: Penguin, 1989.

The Tenant of Wildfell Hall by Anne Brontë, ed. Dr. Stevie Davies, Harmondsworth: Penguin, 2003.
Villette by Charlotte Brontë, ed. Helen Cooper, Harmondsworth: Penguin, 2004.
Shirley by Charlotte Brontë, ed. Lucasta Miller, Harmondsworth: Penguin, 2006.
Jane Eyre by Charlotte Brontë, ed. Margaret Smith, Oxford: Oxford World's Classics, 2008.

BIOGRAPHIES AND SOCIAL CONTEXTS

Oxford Companion to the Brontës, Christine Alexander and Margaret Smith, Oxford: Oxford University Press, 2006.
The Brontës, Their Lives, Friendships and Correspondence, ed. Thomas James Wise and John Alexander Symington, Oxford at the Shakespeare Head Press: Basil Blackwell, 1933. Reprinted by Porcupine Press, Philadelphia, 1980.
Armstrong, Nancy, 'Emily Brontë in and Out of Her Time, *Genre 15*, 1982.
Barker, Juliet R.V., *The Brontës*, London: Weidenfeld and Nicolson, 1994.
Chitham, Edward, *A Life of Emily Brontë*, Oxford: Basil Blackwell, 1987.
Constable, Kathleen, *A Stranger Within the Gates: Charlotte Brontë and Victorian Irishness*, Lanham, MD: University Press of America, 2000.
Eagleton, Terry, *Heathcliff and the Great Hunger: Studies in Irish Culture*, London: Verso, 1995.
Frank, Katherine, *Emily Brontë: A Chainless Soul*, London: Hamish Hamilton, 1990.
Gaskell, Elizabeth, *The Life of Charlotte Brontë*, Harmondsworth: Penguin, 1975.
Gerin, Winifred, *Emily Brontë*, Oxford: Oxford University Press, 1971.
Glen, Heather, *The Cambridge Companion to the Brontes*, Cambridge: Cambridge University Press, 2002.
Gordon, Felicia, *A Preface to the Brontes*, London: Longman, 1989.
Heaton, Emily, *White Windows*, London: Lincoln Williams, 1932.
Ingham, Patricia, *Authors in Context: The Brontës*, Oxford: Oxford University Press, 2006.
Levy, Anita, *Other Woman: The Writing of Class, Race, and Gender 1832–1898*, Princeton: Princeton University Press, 1991.

Lloyd Evans, Barbara and Gareth, *Everyman's Companion to the Brontes*, London: Dent, 1982.

Lonoff, Sue, ed. and trans. *The Belgian Essays: Charlotte Bronte and Emily Brontë*, New Haven: Yale University Press, 1996.

Meyer, Susan, *Imperialism at Home: Race and Victorian Women's Fiction*, Ithaca: Cornell University Press, 1996.

Michie, Elsie B., 'The Yahoo, Not the Demon: Heathcliff, Rochester and the Simianization of the Irish', in *Outside the Pale: Cultural Exclusion, Gender Difference and the Victorian Women Writers*, Ithaca: Cornell University Press, 1993.

Pinion, F. B., *A Brontë Companion*, London: Macmillan, 1975.

Ratchford, Fannie, *The Brontes' Web of Childhood*, New York: Russell & Russell, 1964.

Sneidern, Maja-Lisa, 'Wuthering Heights and the Liverpool Slave Trade', *ELH 62*, 1995.

LITERARY SOURCES AND ASSOCIATED TEXTS

Beddoes, Thomas Lovell, *Death's Jest Book*, Manchester: Fyfield Books, 2003.

Bunyan, John, *The Pilgrim's Progress*, Harmondsworth: Penguin, 2008.

Bunyan, John, *The Life and Death of Mr Badman*, London: Hesperus Classics, 2007.

Byron, George Gordon, 'Manfred', 'Cain', 'The Corsair', 'The Giaour', in *Poetical Works* ed. Frederick Page, a new edition corrected by John Jump, Oxford: Oxford University Press, 1970.

Hogg, James, *The Private Memoirs and Confessions of a Justified Sinner*, Harmondsworth: Penguin, 2006.

Hugo, Victor, *Notre-Dame de Paris*, Oxford: Oxford World's Classics, 2009.

Johnson, Samuel *Prose and Poetry*, London, Rupert Hart-Davies 1950.

Scott, Walter, *Rob Roy*, ed. David Hewitt, Edinburgh: Edinburgh University Press, 2008.

Scott, Walter, *Waverley*, ed. P.D. Garside, Edinburgh: Edinburgh University Press, 2008.

INDIVIDUAL PASSAGES

Passage 4: Yaeger, Patricia, 'Violence in the Sitting Room: Wuthering Heights and the Woman's Novel', *Genre 21*, 1988

Passage 8: 'The rebirth of Catherine Earnshaw: splitting and regeneration of self in *Wuthering Heights*', *Nineteenth Century Studies*, 37–51.

McGuire, Kathryn B., 'The Incest Taboo in Wuthering Heights: A Modern Appraisal', *American Imago* 45, 1988.

Passage 9: Irene Wiltshire, Speech in Wuthering Heights: Joseph's Dialect and Charlotte's Emendations, *Bronte Studies*, 30(1) March 2005.

CRITICAL RECEPTION AND PUBLISHING HISTORY

Alexander, Christine, 'The Art of Emily Bronte', in *The Art of the Brontes*, Cambridge University Press, 1995.

Allott, Miriam, *The Brontes: The Critical Heritage*, London: Routledge and Kegan Paul, 1974.

Allott, Miriam, *Wuthering Heights: A Casebook*, London: Macmillan, 1987.

Armstrong, Nancy, 'Emily Bronté n and Out of Her Time', *Genre 15*, 1982.

Barclay, Janet, *Emily Bronté Criticism 1900 – 1980: An Annotated Check List*, Westport, Connecticut: Meckler Publishing, 1983.

Berman, Jeffrey, 'Attachment and Loss in Wuthering Heights', in *Narcissim and the Novel*, New York: New York University Press, 1990.

Bloom, Harold, *Major Literary Characters: Heathcliff*, New York: Chelsea House Publications, 1993.

Bloom, Harold, *Emily Bronté's Wuthering Heights, Modern Critical Interpretations*, New York: Chelsea House Publications, 2007.

Boone, Joseph Allen, '*Wuthering Heights: Uneasy Wedlock and Unquiet Slumbers*' in *Tradition, Countertradition: Love and the Form of Fiction*, Chicago: University of Chicago Press, 1987.

Buchen, Irving H., 'Emily Bronté and the Metaphysics of Childhood and Love', *NCF XXII*, 1967.

Buckley, Vincent, 'Passion and Control in *Wuthering Heights*', *The Southern Review I*, 1964.

Burns, Bonnie, 'Nostalgia, Apostrophe, *Wuthering Heights*: The Queer Deastiny of Heterosexuality', *Nineteenth-Century Feminisms 1*, 1999.

Cecil, Lord David, *Early Victorian Novelists*, London: Constable, 1934.

Chitham, Edward, *The Birth of Wuthering Heights, Emily Bronté at Work*, London: Palgrave, 2001.

Chitham, Edward, 'Emily Bronté's Latin', *Bronté Society Transactions 21*, 1996.

Cooper-Willis, I., 'The Authorship of *Wuthering Heights*', *The Trollopian II*, 1947.

Craik, W.A:, *The Brontë Novels*, London: Methuen, 1968.

Daley, A. Stuart, 'The Moons and Almanacs of *Wuthering Heights*', *Bronte Society Transactions 21*, 1995.

Daley, A. Stuart, 'A Revised Chronology of *Wuthering Heights*', *Bronte Society Transactions 21*, 1995.

Davies, Stevie, *Emily Brontë: The Artist as a Free Woman*, Manchester: Carcanet, 1983.

Davies, Stevie, *Emily Brontë*, Hemel Hempstead: Harvester Wheatsheaf, 1988.

Davies, Stevie, *Emily Brontë: Heretic*, London: Women's Press, 1994.

Dworkin, Andrea, 'Wuthering Heights', in *Letters from a War Zone*, London: Secker and Warburg, 1987.

Eagleton, Terry, *Myths of Power: A Marxist Study of the Brontës*, London: Macmillan, 1975.

Ewbank, Inga-Stina, *Their Proper Sphere: A Study of the Brontë Sisters as Early Victorian Female Novelists*, London: Harvard University Press, 1966.

Fegan, Melissa, *Wuthering Heights, Character Studies*, London: Continuum, 2008.

Fike, Francis, 'Bitter Herbs and Wholesome Medicines: Love as Theological Affirmation in Wuthering Heights', *NCF XXIII*, 1968.

Gilbert, Sandra and Gubar, Susan, *The Madwoman in the Attic: The Woman Writer and the Nineteenth-Century Literary Imagination*, New Haven: Yale University Press, 1978.

Goodman, Charlotte, 'The Lost Brother, The Twin: Women Novelists and the Male-Female Double Bildungsroman', *Novel: A Forum on Fiction 17*, 1983.

Gordon, Marci M., 'Kristeva's Abject and Sublime in Brontë's *Wuthering Heights*', *Literature and Psychology 34*, 1988.

Hewish, J., *Emily Brontë*, London: Macmillan, 1969.

Holderness, Graham, *Wuthering Heights*, Open Guides to Literature Series, London: Open University Press, 1973.

Homans, Margaret, 'The Name of the Mother in *Wuthering Heights*', in *Bearing the Word*, Chicago: University of Chicago Press, 1989.

Homans, Margaret, 'Repression and Sublimation of Nature in *Wuthering Heights*', *PMLA* 93, 1978.

Jacobs, Carol, 'Wuthering Heights: At the Threshold of Interpretation', in *Uncontainable Romanticism: Shelley, Brontë, Kleist*, Baltimore: John Hopkins University Press, 1989.

Kermode, Frank, 'A Modern Way with the Classic', *New Literary History 5*, 1974.

Kettle, Arnold, *An Introduction to the English Novel,* New York: Harper, 1968.

Knoepflmacher, U.C., *Emily Brontë: Wuthering Heights*, Landmarks of World Literature Series, Cambridge: Cambridge University Press, 1989.

Leavis, Q.D., *'A Fresh Approach to Wuthering Heights'* in *Lectures in America*, Cambridge: Cambridge University Press, 1969.

Lenta, Margaret, 'Capitalism or Patriarchy and Immoral Love: A Study of *Wuthering Heights'*, *Theoria: A Journal of Studies in the Arts, Humanities and Social Sciences 62*, 1984.

Marsh, Nicholas, *Analyzing Texts: Emily Brontë, Wuthering Heights*, London: Macmillan, 1999.

Masse, Michelle A., 'He's More Myself than I Am: Narcissism and Gender in *Wuthering Heights'*, in *Psychoanalyses/Feminisms*, ed. Peter L. Rudnytsky and Andrew M. Gordon, Albany and Buffalo: State University of New York, 2000.

Mathison, John K., 'Nelly Dean and the Power of Wuthering Heights', *Nineteenth-Century Fiction 11*, 1956.

McCarthy, Terence, 'The Incompetent Narrator of Wuthering Heights', *Modern Language Quarterly 42*, 1981.

McGuire, Kathryn B., 'The Incest Taboo in Wuthering Heights: A Modern Appraisal', *American Imago 45*, 1988.

Mengham, Rod, *Emily Brontë: Wuthering Heights*, Penguin Critical Studies Series, Harmondsworth: Penguin, 1988.

Miles, Peter, *Wuthering Heights*, in *The Critics Debate Series*, London: Macmillan, 1990.

Miller, J. Hillis, *The Disappearance of God: Five Nineteenth-Century Writers*, Cambridge: Harvard University Press, 1963.

Miller, J. Hillis, 'Wuthering Heights: Repetition and the Uncanny', in *Fiction and Repetition: Seven English Novels*, Cambridge: Harvard University Press, 1982.

Mitchell, Hayley R., *Readings on Wuthering Heights*, San Diego: Greenhaven Press, 1999.

Moser, Thomas, 'What is the Matter with Emily Jane?: Conflicting Impulses in Wuthering Heights', *Nineteenth-Century Fiction 17*, 1962.

Newman, Beth, 'The Situation of the Looker-on: Gender, Narration, and Gaze in Wuthering Heights', *PMLA 105*, 1990.

Nussbaum, Martha, 'Wuthering Heights: The Romantic Ascent', *Philosophy and Literature 20*, 1996.

Peeck-O'Toole, M, *Aspects of Lyric in the Poetry of Emily Brontë*, Amsterdam: Rodopi, 1988.

Petit, J.-P., *Emily Brontë*, Harmondsworth: Penguin Critical Anthology, 1973.

Pinion, F.B., 'Byron and Wuthering Heights', *Brontë Society Transactions 21*, 1995.

Pinion, F.B., 'Scott and Wuthering Heights', *Brontë Society Transactions 21*, 1996.

Polhemus, Robert M., 'The Passionate Calling: Emily Brontë's Wuthering Heights', in *Erotic Faith: Being in Love from Jane Austen to D.H. Lawrence*, Chicago: University of Chicago Press, 1990.

Pykett, Lyn, *Women Writers: Emily Brontë*, London: Macmillan, 1989.

Ratchford, F., *Gondal's Queen: A Novel in Verse by Emily Jane Brontë*, Austin, University of Texas, 1955.

Robinson, A.M.F., *Emily Brontë*, London: W.H. Allen, 1883.

Sabol, C. Ruth and Todd K. Bender, *A Concordance to Brontë's Wuthering Heights*, New York: Garland, 1984.

Senf, Carol A., 'Emily Brontë's Version of Feminist History', *Essays in Literature 12*, 1985.

Shannon, Edgar F., 'Lockwood's Dreams and the Exegesis of Wuthering Heights, *Nineteenth-Century Fiction 14*, 1959.

Shapiro, Barbara Ann, 'The Rebirth of Catherine Earnshaw: Splitting and Reintegration of Self in Wuthering Heights', in *Literature and the Relational Self*, New York: New York University Press, 1994.

Shorter, C., *Charlotte Brontë and Her Circle*, London, 1896.

Simpson, C., *Emily Brontë*, London: Country Life Ltd, 1929.

Spark, M. and Stanford, D., *Emily Brontë, Her Life and Work*, London: Arena Arrow, 1985.

Spear, Hilda, '*Wuthering Heights by Emily Brontë*', in *Macmillan Master Guides*, London: Macmillan, 1987.

Stoneman, Patsy, *New Casebooks: Wuthering Heights*, London: Macmillan, 1993.

Stoneman, Patsy, *Emily Brontë: Wuthering Heights: A Reader's Guide to Essential Criticism*, Cambridge: Icon Books, 2000.

Tobin, Patricia Dreschel, '*Wuthering Heights: Myth and History, Repetition and Alliance*', in *Time and the Novel: The Genealogical Imperative*, Princeton: Princeton University Press, 1978.

Turner, J. Horsfall, *Haworth, Past and Present*, Brighouse: J.S. Jowett, 1879.

Visick, Mary, *The Genesis of Wuthering Heights*, Hong Kong: Oxford University Press, 1967.

Van Ghent, Dorothy, 'On Wuthering Heights', in *The English Novel: Form and Function*, New York: Rinehart, 1953.

Wallace, Robert K., *Emily Brontë and Beethoven: Romantic Equilibrium in Fiction and Music*, Athens: University of Georgia Press, 1986.

Williams, Raymond, *The English Novel from Dickens to Lawrence*, London: Chatto, 1970.

Wilson, David, 'Emily Brontë: First of the Moderns', *Modern Quarterly Miscellany 1*, 1947.

Yeager, Patricia, 'Violence in the Sitting Room: *Wuthering Heights* and the Woman's Novel', *Genre 21*, 1988.

ADAPTATION, INTERPRETATION AND INFLUENCE

Fanu, Dolores, 'Black and White in *Wuthering Heights*: The Etchings of Rosalind Whitman', *Brontë Studies*, 28, (3), November 2003.

Haire-Sargeant, Lin, 'Sympathy for the Devil: The Problem of Heathcliff in Film Versions of Wuthering Heights', in *Nineteenth-Century Women at the Movies*, New York: Bowling Green University Press, 1999.

Hughes, Ted, *Collected Poems*, London: Faber and Faber, 2003.

Maki Okumura, 'Intrusion of the Stranger: Yoshige Yoshida's Version of Wuthering Heights', *Brontë Studies*, 29, (2), July 2004

Plath, Sylvia, *Collected Poems*, London: Faber and Faber, 1981.

Plath, Sylvia, *Letters Home, Correspondence 1950 – 1963*, London: Faber and Faber, 1975.

Wagner, Erica, Ted Hughes, *Sylvia Plath and the Story of Birthday Letters*, London: Faber and Faber, 2000.

INDEX

149